The Architecture of
Kuwabara Payne McKenna Blumberg

The Architecture of Kuwabara Payne McKenna Blumberg

WITH CONTRIBUTIONS BY

Phyllis Lambert   Detlef Mertins   Bruce Mau   Rodolphe el-Khoury

BIRKHÄUSER – PUBLISHERS FOR ARCHITECTURE
BASEL · BERLIN · BOSTON

Book design: The Office of Kathleen Oginski, Toronto

Project manager: Amanda Sebris, Toronto

Bruce Mau Interview edited by Kyo Maclear

Library of Congress Cataloging-in-Publication Data
The architecture of Kuwabara, Payne, McKenna,
    Blumberg / with contributions by Phyllis Lambert...
    [et al.].
        p. cm.
    Includes bibliographical references.
    ISBN 3-7643-6224-3 (alk. paper)
    1. Kuwabara, Payne, McKenna, Blumberg Architects
    — Themes, motives. 2. Architecture — Ontario —
    20th century. 3. Architecture — Ontario — 21st century.
    I. Lambert, Phyllis.
    NA749.K83A4 2004
    720'.92'2–dc22   2004046287

Bibliographic information published by Die Deutsche
Bibliothek. Die Deutsche Bibliothek lists this publication in the Deutsche Nationalbibliografie; detailed
bibliographic data is available in the Internet at
http://dnb.ddb.de.

© 2004 Birkhäuser – Publishers for Architecture
P.O. Box 133, CH-4010 Basel, Switzerland
Part of Springer Science+Business Media

Printed on acid-free paper produced from chlorine-free
pulp. TCF ∞

Printed in Germany
ISBN 3-7643-6224-3

9 8 7 6 5 4 3 2 1   http://www.birkhauser.ch

Table of Contents

Introduction

by Phyllis Lambert

Architectural studios in which numerous partners have individual practices and yet produce work of high quality and cohesion are a rare phenomenon. KPMB is such a firm. Now a large organization with a staff of eighty-five, making it one of the largest in Canada, it is polymorphic and differentiated rather than pyramidal in structure. In its integrated approach it sets itself apart from the partitioned process of design and production more common to large architectural practices. The individual voices of KPMB partners Bruce Kuwabara, Thomas Payne, Marianne McKenna and Shirley Blumberg are discernible within a common commitment to making appropriate responses to the urban context, to cultivating a strong sense of community, and to producing work for which the art of architecture is the overriding preoccupation.[1] This publication makes these strengths apparent in the built work presented and in the statements made by the four partners. At the same time, specificities of a Canadian practice weave throughout.

The emphasis on the heterogeneity, even disjointedness, of the office structure developed by the four partners is opposed to the singular vision of Barton Myers, in whose office they had all worked together for many years prior to establishing their own studio. When KPMB was formed in 1987, it was unusual in its gender and ethnic make-up as well as its goals. There was no existing model to follow. In addition to producing a consistently high level of work, making a profit was also important so that they could "give back,"[2] assuring growth and personal fulfillment for all who work in the office. A deep level of respect for one another, partners and associates, is evident in their dialogue and keeps them together. Despite individually directed projects, the practice is run as a studio with collaborative involvement and exchange back and forth among team members, including partners who might work together. Despite their collective rejection of Myers' autonomy, his role as mentor is freely acknowledged: "The attitude towards making an appropriate response to the urban context, the use of infill to increase density, enriching the fabric of the city through new/old juxtapositions, creating flexible envelopes to open up architecture during the too-short summer months, creating great rooms within buildings as a response to long winters — this is the legacy of Barton," McKenna states. Having evolved from this position, Kuwabara adds, "the ambition of the practice has grown from these architectural roots."

To an extent that is rare for a major North American architectural practice, much of KPMB's work has comprised additions and renovations to existing buildings. They have turned these commissions, which "draw you into some sort of conversation with what has been there for a longer time," into an opportunity to mould public space. This is so in the much admired Woodsworth College, which was one of the transitional projects marking the emergence of KPMB. Completed in association with Barton Myers, Woodsworth first established KPMB's reputation and reset standards of architectural quality on the University of Toronto campus. The brief to renovate three buildings and to add new classrooms led to a reinterpretation of the academic quadrangle, which also established a coherent urban complex. A highly skillful interweaving of old and new is seen in many of their interior spaces, particularly

at the Design Exchange, Toronto (1994), and St. Andrew's College in Aurora (2003). Even as the firm became more involved in the production of buildings from the ground up, they conceived of them as infill within the city. The Kitchener City Hall has a strong sense of choreographed progression from exterior to interior space, building to the huge city room of the Civic Rotunda. Concordia University in Montréal, to be composed of three separate buildings, is seen as infill in the city on a macro scale, but also as foreground architecture that will establish the university as a major player in the city. Judgment about when a building should be quiet background and when it should be assertive is to me a significant KPMB strength.

The individual identities of the protagonists of KPMB could be observed from the time the firm was formed. In the early built work — retail stores and office interiors — Bruce Kuwabara and Thomas Payne made a great push to consciously establish an elegant architecture with the early retail interior for Marc Laurent (1989). Carefully detailed, finely proportioned with a high level of finish combining wood, glass and metal, and using a restrained palette, the work emanated a certain *élan*, which has since become a signature of the firm.

The other partners describe Kuwabara as incredibly swift, a prolific source of seminal drawings. In all the projects for which he has been design partner, these qualities have evolved and become more architectonically generated — simpler as the projects become larger. This evolution is clearly demonstrated by comparing the complexity of the highly accomplished Kitchener City Hall — an early work in which many ideas were tested — and Centennial College, Scarborough, where as design partner working with a tight budget Kuwabara developed the masterful plan organized in two diverging clear-span arms. Where they intersect at the base of the sloping site, a broad, steeply stepped gathering place — designed to respond to the volume overhead of the enclosed lecture hall — will form an exciting contemporary public space. The elegance of subsuming complex elements into one comprehensible form is found in the Ravine House, where free-standing shapes of

mahogany furniture are resonant of the distinct volumes of the house seen against the horizontal stretch of differentiated ground and ceiling planes.

Over the years, buildings by Payne have become increasingly identifiable as they embody his fascination with the *longue durée*, the building that will still stand five hundred years from now, "with people renovating and occupying it over time," or what Kuwabara terms a commitment to what is "time-honoured." From his schooling on the campuses of Yale and Princeton and at l'École des Beaux-Arts in Paris, Payne retains a deep feeling for historical context, building typologies and morphologies, and expresses a strong desire to create a similar intellectual, emotional, spiritual depth in his own work. This interest first emerged in his use of rusticated stone at Woodsworth College (1991), for which he was partner-in-charge, but where each of the partners' nascent intentions permeate the fabric. Payne's predominant use of masonry and his affinity for Collegiate Gothic became manifest in a major commission, the Joseph S. Stauffer Library at Queen's University, Kingston (1994). A similar vocabulary is found in works such as the Royal Military College at Fort Lasalle, also in Kingston (1997); in the transformation of student residences into research facilities at the Munk Centre for International Studies at the University of Toronto (2000); and inserts itself into the enhancement of Arthur Erickson's Roy Thomson Hall (2002). A robustness of form particular to Payne — and not found in the work of the other partners — is present even in his competition entry, designed with Kuwabara, for a new building on Parliament Hill in Ottawa, as well as in his interior articulations — for example, the solidly bound helical stairs are notable at the Fields Institute, University of Toronto, and at Trinity College Library, Hartford, and, even when they are suspended, at the Joseph S. Stauffer Library, Queen's University, Kingston.

Payne also has developed an active interest in theatre, particularly in understanding the technical requirements, and spatial and material issues related to designing acoustically

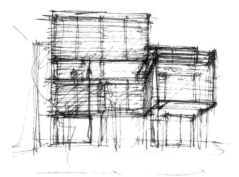

ABOVE: Bruce Kuwabara, early concept sketch of the Gardiner Museum renovation, 2001.

RIGHT: Bruce Kuwabara, competition sketch of the Festival Centre and Tower, 2003.

superior performance space. He has successfully pursued theatre projects, acquiring extensive experience with the Goodman Theatre in Chicago (2000) and Sprague Memorial Hall at Yale University (2003), which has led to the commissions for the Young Centre for the Performing Arts in Toronto (2005), as well as the recently awarded Arthur Miller Theater at the University of Michigan.

Marianne McKenna considers a strong commitment to the program of a building in relation to its community to be a signature of the firm: "We are constantly arguing for the public realm and trying to squeeze as much social space as possible into a building." At the same time, she has pointed to KPMB's dedication "to creating new prototypes, or contemporary paradigms." The firm has met its counterpart in the clients attracted to its orbit. The Grand Valley Institution for Women in Kitchener (1996) provides a stellar example of the coalescence of similar attitudes on the part of client and architect. For new correctional facilities the governmental department, Correctional Services Canada, sought to educate and rehabilitate rather than punish; this was done by creating a community-based environment rather than a place of incarceration. Kuwabara proposed the organizational concept of a common or village green, around which free-standing buildings were structured. McKenna articulated this scheme from the common buildings to the private realm, managing to incorporate 120-square foot porches that were in neither the program nor the budget, but which she felt to be an essential link between cottage and green, private and public. With changes and new demands presented to the architectural team and budget over time, McKenna led the amalgamation of the buildings of common use, which, as in a village model, are marked by a higher level of architectural expression: against the vernacular cottages, the grouping of all the individual buildings into one varied unit focused on the conical form of the ecumenical place of worship and healing is declarative of redemption and community.

As partner-in-charge of the Grand Valley complex, McKenna began to take a more prominent role in the partnership, and her voice has continued to get stronger. McKenna's skill in engaging conversations and interactions with the client, her ability to tease public space from a program and a budget, are evident in projects such as the Jackson-Triggs Niagara Estate Winery (2001) and the new Genomics and Proteomics Research Building in Montréal (2003). The marriage of form and program — with specific reference to the choreography of the visitors' tour through the winery — is characteristic of McKenna. Her declared intention to establish new, environmentally sensitive standards for the wine region through the design of this building is again characteristic of the firm. The integration of the leadership and talents of McKenna and Kuwabara, together with the strong contributions of the project team in the design of the winery, is also characteristic of KPMB's commitment to the collaborative process.

With the Genomics and Proteomics Research Building, the original program was limited to a series of lab and office spaces and McKenna argued to add a series of stacked atrium spaces that link both city and campus, and provide a much-needed social environment for the scientists working in the building. The staircase, for example, extrudes from the west entry through the top four floors, bathed in light from above and extending to the exterior on each floor as a dynamic place where people can meet and interact, and reasserts the belief of the practice that the spirit of a building resides in the social spaces — stairwells, courtyards, cafés — where people can gather and generate a sense of community.

The partnership structure has allowed a play of the different degrees of collaboration amongst the partners. Shirley Blumberg was in charge of certain projects from the mid-1980s to the mid-1990s. In 1986, Blumberg assisted Barton Myers with the first stage of the renovation of a large industrial building for the corporate headquarters of Hasbro in Pawtucket, Rhode Island, and subsequently was partner-in-charge for the successive stages through 1994. Blumberg led the team responsible for transforming the former Toronto Stock Exchange building into the rich, varied interiors of the

ABOVE: Bruce Kuwabara, competition sketch of Vaughan Civic Centre, 2003.

RIGHT: Thomas Payne, working sketch of the Roy Thomson Hall Enhancement, 1999.

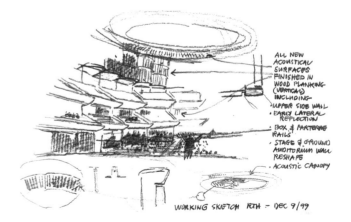

ALL NEW ACOUSTICAL SURFACES FINISHED IN WOOD PLANKING (VERTICAL) INCLUDING
. UPPER SIDE WALL
. EARLY LATERAL REFLECTION
. BOX & PARTERRE RAILS
. STAGE & GROUND AUDITORIUM WALL RESHAPE
. ACOUSTIC CANOPY

WORKING SKETCH RTH — DEC 9/99

Design Exchange. She has increasingly worked closely with Kuwabara, who appreciates her ability to build strong working relationships with clients. They have collaborated since the mid-1990s on the design of corporate offices such as Alias/wavefront and Alliance, and Blumberg has been involved in new projects with him including the Japanese Canadian Cultural Centre, and the new dance training centre for the National Ballet School. As partner-in-charge for the powerfully articulated HP Science and Technology Centre at Centennial College (2004), Blumberg credits the project team for a strong contribution to the design development of the project. The team's concern for environmental issues — ventilation and cladding materials that meet the conditions encountered by the different façades — also demonstrates KPMB's pragmatism in working with tight budgets as well as their increasing preoccupation with sustainable design.

In the last few years, Blumberg and Kuwabara have worked together to push projects towards greater innovation in form, program and expression, particularly evident in recent projects such as the James Stewart Centre for Mathematics at McMaster University in Hamilton (2003), and in the Festival Centre and Tower (2008) for the Toronto International Film Festival Group.

The sense of community that pervades their work distinguishes KPMB's partnership. It is made manifest in their engagement with the public realm, through institutional rather than commercial work, in their collaboration with clients, in their attention to the economy of the studio in order to assure the well-being of the people who work with them, and in their commitment to support institutions and events that raise the profile of the arts and architecture in Canada. KPMB's interest in working with the old and new to conserve and protect involves not only true Canadian conservatism, it also engages a social contract. To me, the strength of architecture in Canada lies in its sense of commitment to a social contract, a contract that has long obtained between the government, the business community and the population with the obligation to create an environment that enhances life and allows individuals to develop to their highest potential.[3]

The partners collectively possess a Canadian consciousness of diversity: "We have always been conscious of our Canadian identity and the fact that Marianne comes from Montréal, Shirley from South Africa, Tom from Chatham, and I [Bruce] from Hamilton. So we come from different places and backgrounds. We think that this is an advantage because it encourages different perspectives."[4] Their work has been concentrated for the most part in Ontario, but while their ambition to extend more broadly into Canada, the United States and Europe is being realized there is an abiding dedication to Toronto where the practice is centred. The obligation to set standards, to raise the quality of art and architecture in Toronto are *leitmotifs* of their discourse and the goal of their built work. The partners deplore that Toronto "has lagged behind other cities in terms of developing high quality architecture."[5] Recent commissions awarded to high profile international architects may change this perception, but the consistently high quality of KPMB's contribution to the architecture of the city has already created the vital synergy that is necessary for new intervention in the urban context.

Notes
1. Quotations are taken from "A Conversation with Bruce Mau," 2 July 2003, in this publication, or communications between myself and the partners.
2. KPMB has made annual donations to a number of cultural organizations. KPMB has also supported the Faculty of Architecture, Landscape & Design at the University of Toronto by contributing to the establishment of the Frank Gehry Chair for International Visitors in Design, and the ongoing building renovations.
3. See Phyllis Lambert, "Canada, Urban Architecture and the Social Contract," McGill Institute for the Study of Canada: The James R. Mallory Annual Lecture in Canadian Studies, McGill University, Montréal, 31 January 2001.
4. Memo Bruce Kuwabara to Phyllis Lambert, 28 August 2003.
5. "Until recently, visitors from around the world have come to Toronto not expecting to see interesting contemporary architectural works. Toronto has lagged behind other cities in terms of developing high quality architecture. George Baird expressed it best when he said that 'Toronto has the best second-rate architecture in the world.'" Memo from Bruce Kuwabara to Phyllis Lambert, 28 August 2003.

MITCHELL HOUSE QUICK SKETCH SOUTH
FOR 18·06·03
KPMB

ABOVE: Thomas Payne, concept sketch of Mitchell House with pool pavilion, 2003.

RIGHT: Thomas Payne, working sketch of Hilton Toronto Vestibule Lobby, 1999.

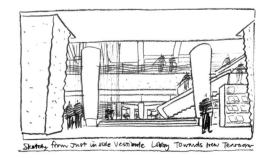

Sketch from just inside Vestibule Lobby Towards new Tearoom

Ravine House, Toronto, 2001.

Toronto Style

by Detlef Mertins

The work of Toronto architects Kuwabara Payne McKenna Blumberg (KPMB) can be situated within the force field of two competing yet interdependent conceptions of style — one normative, the other innovative. Normative style, especially in architecture and art, can refer to established sets of formal conventions, motifs, elements, spatial syntax and material practices which distinguish historical periods, different cultures and the work of specific artists. By contrast, innovative style can refer to someone's manner or *modus operandi*, their way of performing their art, which necessarily involves repetition but simultaneously introduces a crucial difference, thus giving the cultural product the quality of the new. KPMB's way of doing architecture involves both conceptions of style. Their work participates in a widely shared international neo-modernism that constitutes advanced contemporary architecture. Within this, they have developed a personal style that is recognizable yet also elusive because its elements are hybrid and its results tailor-made to the situations and tasks given to them. It is a flexible, "weak" *modus operandi* rather than a strong one, weak in the positive sense of not having predetermined the result in advance. They employ this formal idiom in an open-ended constructive process, generating buildings that are different each time, yet recognizable as the work of one firm. KPMB accept but then manipulate the programmatic, technological and semiotic conventions that society gives its architects, including received conceptions of architectural style and image. They expand the horizon of formal possibilities, but also of experience and activity for those who use their buildings. Their architecture engenders a greater intensity of self-awareness along with a heightened sense of relation to one's surroundings and to others. It stages everyday life in more dynamic and dramatic ways, suggesting a third conception of style as the style of living.

The notion of style as a manner of design that can engender a new way of living has recently been given voice again by the Toronto-based designer Bruce Mau, a compatriot of KPMB. In his book *Life Style* (2000), Mau presents his own increasingly diverse design practice as an alternative to the hardening grip of lifestyle marketing — from Martha Stewart's *Living* to Disney's *Celebration*. For Mau, design actively shapes the world — styles "life" — rather than merely decorating it. Instead of sapping life of its vitality for the sake of a codified repertoire of "creative" activity, as is the case with Martha Stewart's *Living*, Mau proffers that it might be possible — even within a commercial context — to nurture an experimental, transformative and expansive mode of practice not only for the designer but for the user as well.

In the introduction to *Life Style*, theorist Sanford Kwinter — a long-standing collaborator of Mau's and former Torontonian — offers a provocative programmatic statement for such a practice, taking as his point of departure a conception of style announced by Friedrich Nietzsche in the late nineteenth century.[1] Referring to Nietzsche's "aesthetics of existence," Kwinter writes, "All beauty — all power to affect — derives from the way in which things are invested with disposition, how they are made to *appear*." Kwinter tells us that "Nietzsche called this shape-giving aspect of life … 'meaning'…" and "referred to the culminating point of 'meaning' as *style*."

Kwinter emphasizes both the individual — "Nothing is more important, more necessary, 'than to *give style* to one's character' (Nietzsche in *The Gay Science*)" — and the bringing into appearance of the new. Focusing on sports champions and legendary musicians, he suggests that through the articulation of "a single will or viewpoint" it is possible to bring entire systems of novel forms into the world. He proposes that introducing "whole new ways of doing things" realigns our way of being in the world to entirely new rhythmic values: "Think of Jean-Claude Killy's 'avalement' skiing style that brought him three Olympic gold medals and a revolution to the sport ... or in music, of Jimi Hendrix's right thumb."

Extending this performative and transformative theory of style into the design of objects, Kwinter proposes that "design invests raw, even base, matter with 'performativity'," similar yet different from the performance of an extraordinary musician. Design endows inert things with "anima, intelligence and a capacity for action." It makes possible new ways of being in the world. "Design modifies objects so that they, in turn, can modify the world." Design can "quicken the world", animate it, and produce new forms of life with "new rhythmic values." But this would serve no good, Kwinter emphasizes "if it were simply to open the door to new, increasingly sophisticated techniques of human and social engineering." As the modulation of life practices, interactions, rhythms and experiences becomes the focus of economic investment, "to 'give style' to life is, on the contrary, to free life of routine and place it into syncopation so that it can find new, entirely unexpected patterns of unfolding."

Kwinter's conception of style is certainly different and more challenging than that which is common in architecture. It implies not a lexicon of motifs whose deployment serves to re-iterate a codified conception of "modern," "classical," "baroque," or "Victorian" styles — reproducing what is already known without inflection or with only minor reinterpretation. Rather it suggests a unique manner of practising the shared art of architecture and transforming it through innovations in tech-nique, which may then be taken up by others in the field. This *modus operandi* effects change for the user as well as the architect, by opening new domains of experience that enable lives to be lived more expansively and intensely, with "meaning" and style. Considered historically, this model of practice reiterates those of the early twentieth century avant-gardes who sought to achieve change by manipulating and redirecting the systems of production and reception characteristic of emerging mass society. Taking up the new technologies of glass, steel and concrete along with the new media of photography and film, the avant-garde sought to transform them from within, to liberate them from traditions and habits so that they could realize their potential as tools for an emergent society and a new state of consciousness. Kwinter's conception of style combines two moments of avant-gardism which were often at odds — the singular moment of radical actions and events (freedom and creation), which could in principle be ongoing, and the installation of a (new) order, which is collective and systemic in nature and could in principle be durable and unchanging.

Regardless of their differences in political convictions and conceptions of historical change (revolutionary or reformist), modernist architects from the overtly leftist Hannes Meyer, Ernst May and Ludwig Hilberseimer to moderates such as Hugo Häring, Ludwig Mies van der Rohe and Walter Gropius sought to participate in the unfolding of history by developing a new vernacular for a new society, an industrial society already in the making. Drawing on both pre-modern vernaculars and those emerging in industry (such as concrete frame structures for factories), this new language — consider Le Corbusier's Domino or De Stijl's open configuration of planes as exemplars — required a fresh conception of normativity, one that would avoid the rigid pre-determinations associated with the idea of style. This is what the notion of *Gestaltung* or "design" offered. Referring at once to the process of becoming and the resulting form, *Gestaltung* assumed that modern materials and methods of construction constituted a normative system that could be used for the production of difference as easily as it could for the production of uniformity. While we are today accustomed to thinking of early twentieth-century modernism in terms of standardization, seriality and the universalizing repetition of austere technological forms, architects from Frank Lloyd Wright to H.P. Berlage, Hugo Häring and Mies van der Rohe sought to devise a living system of geometry and construction with which to generate an endless variety of building configurations. By accepting standardization for building elements rather than overall forms, each building could be the singular result of the interplay between inner and outer forces, formalizing action rather than motifs.

Despite the contravening efforts of modernists throughout the twentieth century, the historicist conception of style remains alive today in mainstream culture, while dynamic, performative and immanent notions of *Gestaltung* are remembered only among the neo-avant-garde. Modernism itself was assimilated to the idea of an historical style by the 1930s (as "International Style," "Bauhaus Style" or "Modern Style"), and its recent resurgence has largely been taken to be a style with many individual and regional variations.

Toronto Locale

KPMB have repeatedly stressed the importance of the city as a context for their work, both in the physical but also cultural sense. The creative ethos that they have developed — which involves transforming conventions from within — is something that they share with several generations of architects in Toronto. And it is evident in other spheres of activity. Not only have KPMB helped to revise the local modern architecture that emerged in the postwar period, but they have integrated it within the culture of the city at large. KPMB's style is constitutive and exemplary of a Toronto style that is creative and constructive, that stretches the boundaries and begins anew as it affirms continuity and shared values. Over the past three decades, Toronto has become, in every respect, a creative city. As Canada's major financial and cultural centre,

Toronto has become a locus of innovation in business, science and technology, art and design. A relatively young city that became a major centre only after World War II, it is modern through and through, a city-in-the-making, continually intensifying and outgrowing itself. It is robust and entrepreneurial, yet in many ways unselfconscious and even indifferent to its own accomplishments. A city of immigrants — the United Nations has called it the most diverse and multicultural city in the world — it is accustomed to people reinventing themselves within a public framework of tolerance and continuity.

The visual, performing and applied arts all flourish in the city, nourishing new work in art, dance, music, theatre and opera alongside graphic, industrial and furniture design, fashion, advertising, television, radio and film. The city is host to world-renowned festivals in film, video, poetry and new media. It is a city with an extraordinary array of world cuisines, a demanding palette and a host of talented chefs. Over the past decade, the boundary between the fine arts and commercial arts has blurred, giving way to a continuum — an inclusive field of creative activity that nourishes the cultivation of both life and style.

Architecture occupies a significant place in all this, having developed its creative ethos over several generations since the introduction of modernism in the 1950s and 1960s. A handful of local architects had taken up modernist formal innovations prior to the war and had produced some refined works. The modern classicism of Beaux-Art-trained John Lyle in the 1920s, the *moderne* buff-brick buildings of Page & Steele in the 1940s, and the Bauhaus-inspired buildings of Allward & Gouinlock are all landmarks of the first modernist impulses. But modernism in architecture only arrived with gusto after the war, concurrent with the expansion of economy, technology and immigration and the development of a more cosmopolitan social outlook. The international competition for Toronto's New City Hall in 1958 became one of the formative events of that time. Hundreds of entries arrived

LEFT: Toronto City Hall, Toronto, Viljo Revell (1958-64).

RIGHT: Toronto-Dominion Centre, Ludwig Mies van der Rohe with associated architects John B. Parkin and Bregman & Hamann, Toronto (1964-69).

from around the world to be assessed by an international jury led by Eero Saarinen and Ernesto Rogers. Just as Saarinen had steered the selection of the Sydney Opera to the expressionist shells of Jørn Utzon, so in Toronto the jury favoured the futuristic, sculptural symbol of democracy proffered by another Scandinavian architect, Viljo Revell.

In the mid-1960s, the Toronto-Dominion Centre by Ludwig Mies van der Rohe created further momentum for reinvestment in the city centre — its austere modern monumentality introduced a new form and scale of commercial development as well as innovations in technology. It created a city within the city, featuring underground parking, a retail concourse with post office, an observation deck with Inuit art, and serene public spaces both inside and out. If Revell's City Hall fostered a taste for Scandinavian design and an "organic" or "humanistic" modernism, Mies' associates, John B. Parkin Associates, developed a local version of the technically-oriented international style exemplified in America by Skidmore, Owings & Merrill. Peter Dickinson, who arrived in Toronto fresh from the Festival of Britain (1951), created an exuberant personal expression for his projects using shaped and interlocking masses, perforated screens, flying canopies and bubbling fountains. Each in their own way nudged the local construction industry into employing new materials, modes of construction, and building services — into using precast as well as poured-in-place concrete, welded steel frame structures, metal sash windows, aluminum curtain walls, terrazzo floors and air-conditioning. The style of living that they anticipated was active and buoyant, progressive and clean, mutable and aesthetic.

Having placed second in the City Hall competition, the Australian John Andrews relocated to Toronto and established an influential career with "brutalist" projects in the spirit of Team Ten. His Scarborough College for the University of Toronto was a concrete structure with a stepped section and an internal street, situated along the crest of a ravine. Similarly monolithic, his communications needle, the CN Tower,

intended to inaugurate the redevelopment of vast railway lands along the harbour, became the tallest free-standing structure in the world. Eberhard Zeidler also produced several distinguished megastructures, notably Ontario Place (an artificial waterfront of lagoons, pods and bridges), the Eaton Centre (a downtown shopping mall modeled on the galleries of the late nineteenth century), and McMaster Health Science Complex in Hamilton (whose elaborate services run through alternating floors of structure, allowing the occupied floors to be flexible in their arrangement). Raymond Moriyama began his career with a monumental concrete building for the Ontario Science Centre, terracing dramatically down a river valley. During the "heroic" period of Canadian modernism in the 1960s and 1970s, Toronto architects explored the expressive potential of modern materials and methods of construction not only for institutional buildings such as these, but also for a range of generic building types including office towers, apartment slabs, schools and shopping centres. With an emphasis on clear masses, expansive volumes and strong material character, this generation pursued the idea that a new urbanism could be created out of the extension and enlargement of architecture to infrastructural scale.

Modernism Revised

As in Europe and the United States, critiques of modern architecture emerged in Toronto during the late 1970s, focusing on both the destructive urban effects of modern building types and the public's desire for continuity and accessible imagery. In Toronto, the critique of modern urbanism was part of a political reform movement that stopped the construction of downtown expressways and large redevelopments that were devastating entire neighbourhoods. With advocates such as renowned urban theorist Jane Jacobs and two future mayors (David Crombie and John Sewell), the reform movement also included architects Jack Diamond, Barton Myers and George Baird. Diamond and Myers explored low-rise yet high-density alternatives to high-rise towers and slabs, in

LEFT: O'Keefe Centre for the Performing Arts (now Hummingbird Centre), Toronto, Page & Steele Architects, Peter Dickinson, partner-in-charge, 1959-61.

RIGHT: Scarborough College of the University of Toronto, John Andrews, 1964-66.

FAR RIGHT: Barton Myers. A comparative drawing showing the same housing density in several different building configurations and urban morphologies. From "Vacant Lottery," in *Design Quarterly* No. 108 (1978).

order to preserve existing urban fabrics while intensifying them. They developed infill prototypes with courtyards, internal streets and mid-block routes, using geometry and masonry in the manner of Louis Kahn, with whom both had worked. Projects such as York Square (1968–69), Dundas-Sherbourne Housing (1974–76) and Hydro Block Housing (1974–76) became immensely influential for both public and private development, often rendered by other architects in more traditional and decorative guises. Baird, on the other hand, focused on the commercial downtown and suggested ways to ameliorate the negative effects of free-standing towers by adding podia, arcades and public routes to improve the micro-climate and to endow privately owned spaces with a public character. He also advocated buildings that combined different uses and provided multiple levels of public activity as ways to temper mono-functionalism and introversion.

Working with students at the University of Toronto in the late 1970s, Baird extended this revisionist modernism by importing the analytical tools of urban morphology and typology developed in Europe by Aldo Rossi, Maurice Culot, Bernard Huet, Fernado Montez, O.M. Ungers and others — which had been presented to North American readers in the New York-based journal *Oppositions*.[2] At the same time, the recuperation of Russian constructivism, most notably in London, also found its way to Toronto and became a second powerful influence for this generation and the next. Colin Rowe's critique of modernist urbanism and his contextual and collagist approach to urban design were also formative for Toronto architecture in the late 1970s and early 1980s. Collage or assemblage offered a formal paradigm capable of bridging urban and architectural scales and was open to a diverse range of formal and stylistic idioms, from the mannerist Corbusianism of the New York Five to the neo-constructivism of James Stirling and Rem Koolhaas, on the one hand, and the neoclassicism of Leon Krier and Michael Graves, on the other, all of who enjoyed significant followings in Toronto.

This revision of modernism also addressed symbolic issues. Robert Venturi's critique of modern architecture as culturally reductive and out of touch with public tastes (*Complexity and Contradictions*, 1968) launched many efforts to mutate and hybridize modern forms so as to evoke pre-modern styles and the vernaculars of popular culture while remaining abstract. In Toronto, Baird's early work on semiotics and public culture sensitized his colleagues and students to the shared nature of meaning in architecture, while emphasizing the performative and open dimensions of language rather than the codification of signs and styles.[3] During the late 1970s and early 1980s, Baird developed a collagist approach to renovating and extending existing buildings, indebted to the hybridity of Carlo Scarpa with projects such as Castelvecchio Verona, begun in 1956. Scarpa's work also influenced Myers, although Myers adopted pre-modern typologies, figuration and decorative patterns in a simpler and more straightforward way. Articulate assemblage — from the largest scale of the building down to the smallest detail — allowed these architects to redirect the modernist pursuit of material expression toward more figural and communicative ends. By enriching their palette of materials, textures, colours and techniques of fabrication, they transformed modernist abstraction into a tectonic poetics capable of winning over a public whose tastes were conditioned by the decorative and material complexity of historical styles.

KPMB Style

KPMB's way of doing architecture — their style — emerged out of this mixture of extensions, critiques and correctives to late modernism, which involved transforming and merging various precedents, local and international, historical and contemporary. Having apprenticed initially with other architects — Kuwabara and Payne, for instance, both worked with Baird for several years — the future partners of KPMB had all been with Myers for between seven and twelve years before starting their firm (1987). More than Myers, however, they

treated the entire history of modernism and the global field of contemporary practice as a reservoir to draw from, developing their work by looking backwards and extending forward. In the process they turned modern architecture into a heterogeneous and versatile medium with which to respond to varied situations and expectations. Theirs is not a reductive formal language nor a mechanical repetition of forms, but rather a practice that draws on a broad repertoire of formal, spatial and technical devices in order to produce distinctive and situated works.

For their first major independent commission, the Kitchener City Hall (1989–1993), KPMB combined a low U-shaped building, which frames the streets and civic square in red sandstone, with a glass and steel tower reminiscent of commercial office buildings but smaller, more monumental and dynamic. They inserted an abstracted rotunda into the base to serve as a lobby and event space, and floated an exuberant metallic canopy over the entrance, resembling more the wing of an airplane than a part of a conventional building. Part neo-rationalist, part constructivist, and part machine-age, this assemblage achieved a legible whole while its parts remained discrete and compositionally unintegrated. It was tied together by consistencies in detailing and a syntax that elaborated components without articulating joints, from window frames to handrails, cladding to interior paneling. Internally, long views within the podium linked its public spaces and prompted movement between them, elaborating the perception and image of the building through experience. With a more everyday program, the mixed-use office and retail complex King James Place (1991) sensitively filled in two empty lots around existing historical buildings along one of the main commercial streets of nineteenth-century Toronto. A variety of projects for different universities have likewise extended the traditions and morphologies of the university campuses, in some instances amalgamating older buildings and in all cases giving new shape and meaning to public spaces. For instance, Woodsworth College at the University of Toronto (1991) brings together brick, stone, wood and metal in a hybrid character with multiple stylistic resonances as it creates a new quadrangle that incorporates a Victorian House and Drill Hall. More boldly, the McGill University Genomics and Proteomics Research Building in Montréal (2003) inserts a rectangular prism of glass and steel (refined in colour, pattern and translucency) between buildings of different generations, neatly fitting into the context while departing from it and giving increased definition and meaning to the street and internal campus. Unlike many firms of their size, KPMB also renovate existing buildings, including landmark buildings such as the Design Exchange (1994) and Roy Thomson Hall (2002), both in Toronto. For the Hilton Hotel in Toronto (2000) they updated the standard formats of lobbies and hotel rooms with a rich array of elements — differentiated yet complementary in shape, material and light — brought together in a generous and understated elegance.

Just as Le Corbusier and Mies adapted and transformed vernacular architectures, both industrial and pre-modern, so too does KPMB, albeit focusing on late twentieth-century office buildings, corporate interiors, and retail formats as well as civic squares, collegial quadrangles and houses. Having abandoned the modernist quest for universal forms, which were to be appreciated in themselves, they render these North American vernaculars with a complexity that engages the culture of their occupants, speaking to the senses as well as to the longing for image. While the Grand Valley Institution for Women in Kitchener (1996) works with domestic as well as institutional forms, the Jackson-Triggs Niagara Estate Winery in Niagara-on-the-Lake (2001) evokes barns and wineries both local and European. In a more corporate register, the prototype designs for the Ammirati Puris Lintas Offices (1997) and Star Alliance Airport Lounges (2001) develop what amounts to a vernacular within the genre of offices and lounges for global clients. By orchestrating activities, movements and affects of character, atmosphere and style, KPMB mediate experiences and restructure the relationship of

LEFT: York Square, Toronto, A. J. Diamond, Architect, and Barton Myers, 1968-69. An important precedent for the retention of existing fabric and the creation of new urban spaces.

RIGHT: George Baird. A drawing from Baird's section of "Vacant Lottery" in *Design Quarterly* No. 108 (1978) showing how a tower or slab can be urbanized with a base or podium or other contextual inflection.

occupants to their surroundings — be it a city street, a campus or a park landscape — to one another and to themselves.

Working closely with their clients and concretely in each situation, KPMB uses the idiom that they have collectively developed to create a family resemblance among singular buildings, each of which expresses a specific nexus of shaping forces and opportunities. These forces, like KPMB's architecture, are in part generic and in part individuated. Able to customize the quotidian, they create expressions of diversity within the everyday that result from the interaction of many formative factors. They respond creatively to a diverse array of clients, situations, programs, contexts, scales, budgets and audiences with a typology of elements and a set of techniques that lend the work consistency. The range of KPMB's work is understood not in a limited sense of program but in an expanded sense of audience and context. Each project brings with it a different set of societal expectations as well as a unique physical setting. Different locations and contexts, in Canada and abroad, also inflect the projects, in form as in materials and methods of construction. Yet another dimension of the diversity of their work comes from the partners, each of whom deploys the firm's formal and technical idiom in somewhat different ways.

Underpinning this propensity for diversity is a formalism that is neither idealist nor essentialist and whose results are neither standardized nor predetermined by an idea. Instead, one sees a looser materialist formalism, a constructive formalism of means, or, better, a constructive system that consists of a repertoire of forms, elements, combinatorial logics and material practices. While they use off-the-shelf components and products, these are combined into architectural elements — walls, ceilings, canopies, screens, stairs, rooms, windows, etc. — that are themselves not prefabricated. Rather they constitute types that can be customized and localized each time. They are open to re-interpretation as the architects assemble matter into figures of order and shape. These buildings become unique through the interplay of inner and outer

forces. Mediated by a system of design and construction that is inclusive and adaptable, the results resonate both with one another and with their social and physical *milieux*.[4]

KPMB's system differs from its modernist antecedents on numerous fronts. Foremost among these is KPMB's hybridity and readiness to address taste cultures that were excluded from the *ideology* of modernism, even if, today, we know that they often found their way surreptitiously into modernist *practices*. In their hybridity, KPMB follow the lead of Pierre Chareau's idiosyncratic fusions in the Maison de Verre more than the systemic rigours of De Stijl, Le Corbusier's purism, Bauhaus orthodoxy or the International Style epitomized by Skidmore, Owings & Merrill — although they draw on all of these as sources. In addition to accepting an expanded field of cultural references and engaging the process of semiosis through the combination of figuration, abstraction and construction, KPMB achieve hybridity and complexity through a proliferation of materials and methods of construction. Unlike the mono-materiality of Brutalist concrete or Miesian steel, KPMB's heterogeneous assemblages employ a broad array of materials, finishes and fabrication techniques. Most of their buildings use concrete slab structures, which in themselves provide flexibility and adaptability. Finding the tolerance for adaptation, innovation and individuation within the North American building industry, they use standard products and methods of construction in non-standard as well as standard ways. But their work also incorporates custom fabrication and craft elements for selected smaller scale elements, especially those involving metalwork, millwork and lighting. It is the design of these fine details that imbues their buildings with distinctive character and makes them appeal so strongly to the senses, pleasing the eye and evoking the impulse to touch. Their early experience with retail interiors such as Marc Laurent (1986–1991), brought them into contact with highly skilled trades people in Toronto, often immigrants who have maintained craft traditions using modern as well as traditional materials in specialty metal and woodshops.

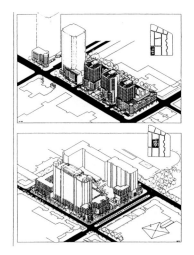

KPMB have developed a composite and customized modernism that works within and against the grain of mainstream construction, budgets and tastes. Their constructive style can be tuned and adapted to suit any occasion. Versatile and flexible, responsive to local conditions, traditions and desires, it enables them to produce buildings that stand out while fitting into their context. Their buildings can be more heterogeneous or homogeneous, more symbolically charged or more abstract, expensive or inexpensive, dramatic or recessive, elegant or severe. This hybridity differentiates their work from corporate practices that cater to public acceptance with either eclectic or generic formulas. KPMB's eclecticism, if it may be called that, differs from the historicism of the nineteenth century and its contemporary reiterations precisely in its lack of purity, its resistance to doctrinaire codification, and its ability to generate symbolic resonances through abstract form and tectonic expression. Working in the manner of a commercial practice, they avoid its limitations and formulas by combining invention with realism, creating buildings that are extraordinary as well as ordinary, localized and individuated. While indebted to the experiments of the historical avant-garde, their architecture is moderate, not extreme, tasteful and appropriate rather than challenging or alienating. The newness that they achieve does not produce revolution, but rather works transformatively to open up horizons of expression and experience.

If, on the one hand, KPMB's work is accommodating of societal norms and conventions, it also departs from them to create new opportunities for the ways in which their clients and inhabitants live. Their buildings are not objects in themselves, to be appreciated or consumed as such, but rather open constructions that invite participation and set the stage for experiences, activities and pleasures that are not found in mainstream architectural production. In their public spaces, they introduce openness where closure is the norm, they offer material texture and tactility where blandness prevails, connective views and sequences of movement that relate inside and outside, public and private, at the same time that they link internal activities and uses to one another. And they introduce materials, colours, textures, effects of light, translucency and reflectivity that engender a heightened sense of perception and attunement to one's surroundings — to changes in the day, in weather and the seasons, to the flow of people and events.

Perhaps most telling of all, KPMB introduces public spaces where often none are provided — spaces for everyday use but also special events. These spaces are theatrical settings for both programmed and unprogrammed events. They are multifunctional and suggestive without determining activity in any rigid sense. Much of KPMB's energy goes into the design of these spaces — into street edges, elevations and entrances, public squares, courtyards and gardens, lobbies, passages and assembly rooms. They understand that these are the settings in which life and history unfold and therefore give them distinctive material character and special elements such as fountains, towers and canopies. Orchestrating views and movement in relation to these spaces intensifies their role as dramatic settings, be it the civic square at Kitchener, the quadrangle at Woodsworth College or the lobby of the Hilton Hotel in Toronto. Even their houses stage activities and events either by the power of reductive abstraction (Reisman-Jenkinson Residence, 1991), or by means of shifting levels, opening and closing vistas, and articulating thresholds (Ravine House, 2001). In manifold ways, their buildings engender a sense of expectancy, of living in the present, of being attuned to the singularity and potential of the moment.

The recent evolution of their work reinforces this expectant temporality, as the tone of their buildings has shifted from hot tectonic mixtures to cool surface mutations which recede into the background, allowing activities and perceptual affects to take even greater precedence over visual signification. The restrained elegance and generous sophistication of the Ravine House (2001), the Star Alliance Lounge (2001), and the forthcoming HP Science and Technology Centre for Centennial College, supports a style of living in which bodies ambulate in rhythmic sequences that are slower than usual. Stimulated by fine materials, dramatic lighting, flowing spaces and crisp edges, occupants may experience a heightening of senses — in the same manner that conversation may be invigorated by fine foods, opening up spaces for reflection, dialogue and action.

KPMB have been a catalyst in Toronto for developing a neo-modern style that goes beyond our expectations of how a style performs, beyond the signifying effects of style. Drawing on the work of an older generation and in turn mentoring a younger one, they have helped pioneer a distinctive way of doing architecture whose effects are adventurous while operating within mainstream culture.[5] KPMB have transformed the architectural culture that they inherited. They completed the shift from universalizing megastructures to intensifications of the city that respect urban conventions while moving beyond them to articulate specific situations and mark differences. Considered in historical context, KPMB's *modus operandi* has helped change the art of architecture in Toronto, spawning a versatile, adaptable and culturally inclusive modernist vernacular capable of intensifying experience and expanding the horizons of life.

Notes

1. Sanford Kwinter, "The Gay Science: What is Life?" in Bruce Mau, *Life Style* (New York/London: Phaidon, 2000): 35–37. Kwinter's introduction helps frame Mau's confrontation with the contemporary phenomenon of life style as a normative set of images, artifacts and practices mobilized by corporations hoping to colonize consciousness in today's hyper-mediatized economy.

2. See Barton Myers and George Baird, guest eds., "Vacant Lottery," *Design Quarterly*, No. 108 (1978).

3. Together with Charles Jencks, Baird co-edited *Meaning in Architecture* (London: Design Yearbook, 1969; New York: George Braziller, 1970). Baird's writings during the 1970s and 1980s emphasized conceptions of the public that explored the implications of the philosophy of Hannah Arendt for architecture and urbanism. Baird's writings culminated in the book, *The Space of Appearance* (Cambridge: MIT Press, 1995).

4. This is the kind of formalism that Kwinter implies when he says that "true formalism is any method that diagrams the proliferation of fundamental resonances and demonstrates how these accumulate into figures of order and shape." See Sanford Kwinter, "Who's Afraid of Formalism?" *ANY* (7/8): 65.

5. The Toronto Society of Architects recently published a *Guide Map to Toronto Architecture 1953–2003*, which presents a multi-generational genealogy of the interwoven careers through which a new modernism has emerged in Toronto.

A Conversation with Bruce Mau

Bruce Kuwabara   Thomas Payne   Marianne McKenna   Shirley Blumberg

BRUCE MAU: I want to focus on two quite different aspects of your practice:

The first is your cultural project or ambition; the true purpose of your work as it affects your own lives individually but also as partners and collaborators, as citizens and as historical characters.

The second is the apparently mundane day-to-day function of the business: the infrastructure of your project.

The relationship between these two realms has always been for me the most perplexing to negotiate; that internal relationship between vision and infrastructure, between ambition and practice. In my experience, the degree to which the infrastructure is a projection of the ambition often determines the degree to which the vision is realized.

Personally, I'm always fascinated by the way people work and how they manage.

So let's begin with the first (your cultural project or ambition), and we'll swing back and forth between these two separate sets of questions.

The first question is in some ways the most personal: how would you define your own project? What is obvious now is that you are assured of a place in the history of architecture in Toronto and Canada and more and more internationally. You are at a certain moment in your practice. What is it that you want to do now? What are your aspirations? Not necessarily in terms of the business, but what do you want to achieve for yourself and how do you see your project in a broader civic sense?

BRUCE KUWABARA: The project, which is the practice, begins with our formation as an "uneasy and complex hybrid,"[1] and embraces the question of how that hybrid condition might serve as an artistic model in the world. There are very few firms structured quite like ours. When we founded our practice, we had an opportunity to set the terms of a different model of practice than the ones employed by our predecessors, most of whom were masters directing pyramidal offices. Our model began differently, interacts differently, and produces a less assimilable kind of work. In this regard, it is difficult to generate an easy or homogeneous reading of KPMB.

THOMAS PAYNE: Some potential clients are looking for a singular *Gestalt*, or a commodified architectural expression where the signature is immediately recognizable. Our work is not so simple to read. And so as we move forward into the next phase of our work, as we compete for international commissions, it will be an interesting challenge to strengthen our identity.

BRUCE KUWABARA: The practice is complex artistically—especially when you consider authorship, identity, branding and all those issues that are about the competitive nature of design. But we began by trying to do something different. It was about establishing a quality of life and practice that would be different than what we had each experienced before.

MARIANNE MCKENNA: It is interesting to think of our history. The four of us began as associates working for Barton Myers.[2] Barton left Toronto in 1987, and we carried on as a team. I think our original model for practice has evolved but we've sustained the ethnic and gender diversity that was the hallmark of our studio at the time we started up. There were no architectural firms with two men and two women as partners, with all four principals leading projects.

BRUCE KUWABARA: In terms of a contemporary practice our gender and ethnic diversity resonates with how the rest of Canada is operating. I think our work in its complexity and apparent disjointedness has its own identity, its own coherence. Sometimes it is hard for us to brand ourselves except through discussions like this—that challenge us to consider why our work has this interplay and complexity.

SHIRLEY BLUMBERG: We came out of a studio that was very much about a singular vision. Barton Myers had a very systematic approach to design that had its origins in the work of Louis Kahn — but the expression of his buildings also referenced Charles Eames' approach to detailing and materials. We spoke about our vision at length when we started our practice. We searched for existing models of practice that would be an example for us but we could not find any. What is more typical in practice is to have separate partners in charge of design, management, production and marketing. We were all very much hands on, directly focused on the development of the projects.

A healthy instability, I think, has characterized the practice. We don't compartmentalize the process into design and production. That continuity enables us to think about every aspect of a project although it's not always the most efficient way to do things.

When John Ralston Saul's book *Reflections of a Siamese Twin* came out in 1997, he spoke about the complexity and heterogeneity of Canadian identity. It struck us more and more that the phenomenon he was describing was in fact an intrinsic part of the culture of our firm.[3]

BRUCE KUWABARA: His argument is that Canada is one of the most engaging contemporary models of democracy in the world. When I read the book it resonated with my personal experience, as well as that of the practise. Saul argues that it is not just the primary Native, English and French cultures that make up Canada but that Canada has always been strongest when it recognizes its richer condition of hybridization.[4]

MARIANNE MCKENNA: I think the cultural project of our practice began with understanding the city, initially in the context of Toronto.

Our training was heavily influenced by Barton Myers and George Baird[5] (for whom both Bruce and Tom worked prior to joining Barton). The attitude towards making an appropriate response to the urban context, the use of infill to increase density, enriching rather than dumbing-down the fabric of the city through new/old juxtapositions, creating flexible envelopes for buildings to open up during our too-short summer season and great indoor spaces to compensate for our long, hard winters — this is the legacy of Barton. We've evolved from that position; and I would say that the ambition of the practice has grown from these architectural roots.

THOMAS PAYNE: In the firm there are various creative axes. Like music, you become good at playing with particular people. It is like improvisational jazz where you can't presume that you can randomly put teams together to play the music, or in our case, to do the work. People play complementary roles; there are specific synergies that work. In my case, I've worked a lot with Chris Couse, a senior associate, and Goran Milosevic, an associate.

BRUCE KUWABARA: Part of our cultural agenda emerges from a belief that from a very local situation it is possible to produce something of a very high calibre. I think a lot of people who visit Toronto and see our projects are delighted and surprised to find a high level of work going on. Maybe it's just something that we've been trying to prove. You [Bruce Mau] have proven it big time in the field of design but from an architectural point of view our ambition has been to produce work that can be appreciated at any time, anywhere in the world. Our office may be in Toronto, but we are doing things elsewhere. That is what we want our work to communicate — as a declaration of quality.

MARIANNE MCKENNA: We don't take a singular position, but respond to the program, the community of users, the context, and also our desire to create a distinctive and sustainable idea for every project. The strategy is consistent, but the solutions come from thinking through the problems as they are presented.

BRUCE KUWABARA: We spend a lot of time on our work.

THOMAS PAYNE: We can also be extremely fast. Sometimes you have to be lightning quick, especially when generating ideas and the first image.

We've talked about the heterogeneity of expression. Some projects are incredibly dense in detail, and perhaps technically complex and difficult to build, while others are simpler and more straightforward. Often this contrast occurs within a single project.

SHIRLEY BLUMBERG: And I think the projects are also aspirational. What we did at the beginning was establish that we would not change our approach for what is called bread-and-butter work — everything would count, no matter what we took on.

BRUCE KUWABARA: We invest a great deal of energy at every phase of every project in the details. One thing that distinguishes our office is that the process is not partitioned. Typically, the split in an architectural firm is between design and production. One of our first objectives was to unify the process. We form a team and the team goes right through concept, design, design development, contract documents and, finally, construction. We may buttress it at times, but the guiding principle is distinctive from firms which hand over the design to a separate production department.

MARIANNE MCKENNA: We couldn't do the work we do that way.

BRUCE MAU: Why not?

BRUCE KUWABARA: We would lose a lot in the translation.

MARIANNE MCKENNA: We go to interviews with the team of key people who will be working on the project. They are involved in the idea of the project and the guiding principles that we establish with the client at the outset. There is a language that evolves from these sessions. It wouldn't work to take all of that information at the end of, say, design development, and hand it to production people to do working drawings. The language moves through these phases and evolves right through shop drawings, and sometimes even on the construction site, where you see things that aren't quite right and race to change them, or see opportunities to enhance a project, and act immediately. We tell clients right from the start that this is the way we work.

When we finished the Grand Valley Institution for Women,[6] George Centen, who was part of the original client group representing Correctional Services Canada, came on site at the completion of the project. Afterwards, he told me that ours was the only project — out of five regional facilities that were built — that had maintained its original vision. I don't think you can have that kind of continuity by passing the project off to other hands.

SHIRLEY BLUMBERG: For it to work, it is very important that everyone on the team understands the founding thesis of the project; that every decision that is made in detailing, for example, follows the main thrust of the original idea. Everyone on the team should understand where to place the emphasis in the architecture — which elements are important, which are not.

BRUCE KUWABARA: The theory is that you have a staff that is well-rounded and intelligent.

They have design capability but also a technical interest.

THOMAS PAYNE: The one qualifier I would add is that in practice, while some of the very best designers can do production work well, there are occasions when it is necessary to find support in translating the design into built form, especially in the case of bigger, more complex commissions. The term Bruce used was "buttress." We would love to have an office of generalists alone — and that is the way we started — but now we also have a few key people, a few gems, who have a knack for digging in and dealing with the technical complexity of larger projects, and who ensure that the buildings will have longevity.

BRUCE MAU: In my studio, we are also confronting the question of how much to specialize. We have a concept of "everything teams" where each team has the capacity to produce everything the studio does but we are also realizing that we need a localized focus so that each group would have the capacity to do it all, but also the capacity to focus on a particular aspect of the practice.

It is interesting, this notion of "the team," the strength in the group you mentioned. Bill Buxton[7] spoke with me about a concept that he referred to as the "Renaissance Team." In fact, he explained that it is not plausible today to produce a Renaissance character but it is possible to produce a Renaissance team. In other words, it is possible to put a group together that collectively has the strength that no single individual could ever have.

One thing that I know from my discussions with other architects, who you earlier referred to as your "predecessors," is that there is a certain amount of suspicion of the collective in the field. I struggle with this all the time because, of course, I have a studio of thirty-five people who are all

incredibly creative producers. All of our work is collaborative work. I can't imagine something that I've done by myself. But still there is an obsession with the singular, and the individual character, in our culture and especially in the field of architecture.

MARIANNE MCKENNA: There is an interesting book that inspired us when we launched into designing the first three prototypes for Heather Reisman's Indigo bookstore venture. It was a management text about leadership called *Organizing Genius*, and it described the characteristics of great leaders who worked with a talented team to create monumental advancements in their particular fields.[8] The book described what it takes to lead a team of collaborators beyond the first "big idea" and to realize the objective.

We go beyond the initial concept through a collaborative adventure with our staff. It is our role to maintain the vision, buffer the team from discouraging downturns and cajole the very best from everyone involved. Part of our task is to help these individuals grow and to realize their capacity within the constraints of a project.

I think we've all evolved into strong leaders in terms of the Renaissance teams you mention. The people that we work with have top-rate skills and boundless creativity, and we have been lucky to have this core team of dedicated people who also contribute a high level of professionalism and technical skill.

BRUCE MAU: Do you work as masters? Is it a studio of four masters?

BRUCE KUWABARA: The master model would relate to the other paradigm we discussed. Our role is more that of mentors, advocates and leaders, in the sense that Marianne described.

THOMAS PAYNE: We use the expression "genius of collaboration" but then we also recognize that virtually every project is initiated by a spark that comes out of an individual's mind; generating the idea—what Barton called the "Big Idea"—is what propels the project, especially in the early moments, and sustains it throughout.

BRUCE KUWABARA: There is genius, there is the "genius of collaboration," and then there is just collaboration. Genius is rare. Sometimes it is a brief instant of creative imagination.

I'd be curious in your practice [Bruce Mau] whether or not the greatest proportion of "big ideas" come almost immediately after your initial analysis of the problem. I think the forms of leadership we are discussing are similar—i.e. someone has an idea that can come into the world only after a certain gestation period, and after considerable labour. Someone said 1% inspiration, 99% perspiration, and Robert Venturi said 10% design and 90% problem-solving. For us, architecture is a lot of hard work. The sheer amount of functional, engineering and technical development is enormous. That is why we want continuity from beginning to end. A lot of buildings can start out with a really great idea, but they don't necessarily translate into reality. Carlo Scarpa said there are no good ideas, only good expression. I always ask my students: "So what does that mean?"!

In architecture it means a lot. If the original spark, or concept, is not there in the final built work, it's just not there. It cannot be resurrected after the fact.

THOMAS PAYNE: So, while much of our work begins with an idea and a vision of the building's expression, it is also coupled with a very clear conception of technique and of how things are to be built. Ideally, when the idea for a project is launched, it has been considered simultaneously from many vantage points.

BRUCE KUWABARA: But I would also add that some of our projects grope their way into the world. They don't just go "thump" and come out whole.

I think our best work took us a long time because we struggled with it.

MARIANNE MCKENNA: That is where the collaboration of the team is incredibly valuable, because there is a huge amount of exploration in the group. That is the role of the leader—to look at what you are groping towards to maintain the distinctive aspects of the project, to uphold value for the client…

SHIRLEY BLUMBERG: …to determine what is useful and what is not…

BRUCE KUWABARA: …and to try to distill what is essential.

But do we have a system?

THOMAS PAYNE: There was a time when we were very closely aligned with how Barton practised. He was a strong mentor figure. This was natural. But I believe we are an extremely heterogeneous group and good original thinkers, and so we've started to explore other approaches, finding our own particular creative grooves. For example Barton always began with the "Big Idea" and "Planning the Plan," which we still do. And he researched things as we do, but I think we've evolved a stronger affinity with the client and "the genius of collaboration."

There are certain methodologies that are beneficial or necessary in moving a project a certain distance with a minimal amount of discussion, and there are others which enable a project to morph and mutate, to "grope" its way more gradually.

BRUCE KUWABARA: You have to observe the project closely and see what is happening with the work itself. Sometimes you discover the idea as you are "groping" your way forward.

THOMAS PAYNE: The process can be slow or fast. There are surprises. Sometimes a junior member of the team will change the direction of the project.

BRUCE MAU: That raises one of the most interesting questions, in my opinion. You know, when I think about your studio and how it operates with so many people and four directors, one of the first things that preoccupies me is the question of style. There are two models that one can imagine: the first is that people begin to understand the style of the office and go on to produce in this mode. In the second scenario, there is a problem-solving method and the style emerges in a way out of that process. There are many studios where there is an absolutely definitive style to the point of fixed presentation material. A client entering into that process simply gets in line and pays their fee. In other studios — for instance, my own — there isn't a house style. There is a culture that produces a method, and the method produces objects and images that can have virtually any manifestation — a public park, a book, an exhibition…

BRUCE KUWABARA: I think that our practice sits between those two models. Some people say that there really is a KPMB-ism, or a style that signifies KPMB. The truth of the matter is that your own design, that of Bruce Mau Design, may institutionalize itself as a brand, whether you like it or not, because you have produced a number of projects, and people are looking for common threads in order to identify a body of work or establish a "signature." That is what people do.

MARIANNE MCKENNA: A signature of our work is a focus on *the program* of a building in

relation to the community it will eventually accommodate and, ideally, cultivate. For any project we take on we try to identify the relevance of the program, beyond a list of spatial requirements.

Clients also come to us with the challenge to create new prototypes — when they do not want what the marketplace is dishing out. The Grand Valley Institution is an example. Correctional Services, the client, wanted to transform the incarceration pattern. The Providence Centre, a centre for the aged, was the same: the government was changing the model for how the frail elderly were housed in Ontario and the objective was to move away from an institutional to a residential model. Similarly, Indigo broke down the conventional paradigm of big box retail into a series of intimate, social spaces to encourage book lovers to spend time browsing.

THOMAS PAYNE: Our work is heterogeneous in expression. All of it aspires to be *of this time*. Yet we are also building *for all time*. So, why would anyone construct a building out of masonry today? Maybe because of the location, the client brief, where the building is in the world. We consider the *longue durée*. We imagine a building being here five hundred years from now, with people renovating and occupying it over time.

I am personally fascinated by the idea of longevity. I think that it is an important part of our practice, the belief in the continuity of architecture and what it brings to culture, and society. Unlike some other artistic disciplines, architecture is out there, exposed to the weather, taking a permanent place in the world. Once a building has been detailed and contracted for construction you can't easily edit it, you can't pull it off the shelf, sometimes you can't even touch it. The expectation in the institutional realm is that, as an architect, one builds with an eye to enduring value, turning over to the client something that will stand the test of time.

SHIRLEY BLUMBERG: One of the biggest challenges after decades of practice is how to keep our work fresh. In my view, that is the real value of working in a large complex studio such as ours, with the stimulation of different teams and a broad range of project types.

When Alias/Wavefront[9] selected us to design their studios, they requested that their project not resemble anything we had done before. That was a welcome challenge. We have always delighted in opportunities like that which push us to develop different expressions in the work. It keeps our studio vital.

BRUCE MAU: How big do you think the studio can get?

SHIRLEY BLUMBERG: Not much bigger …

BRUCE MAU: You don't see it as a cellular model that could simply replicate?

MARIANNE MCKENNA: No, because the studio's success lies in the strength of the individuals. We have such talented, strong collaborators among the associates and the project architects, and really all the individuals who work here in this rather idiosyncratic culture. Most of the people here stay because they are very involved with the projects and appreciate the work we get to do, and the culture of the office.

BRUCE MAU: How many people currently work here?

BRUCE KUWABARA: Eighty-five.

BRUCE MAU: When you think about it as the combined total of four amalgamated studios, working with four leaders, it's actually not that big.

BRUCE KUWABARA: I don't think it is a size issue as much as it is about the people who compose the organization. There are firms that are larger than ours that produce extraordinarily strong work.

THOMAS PAYNE: Another consideration is that we are involved in a variety of joint ventures so the actual manpower figure is probably greater. The number might be closer to one hundred and fifty.

BRUCE KUWABARA: When you [Bruce Mau] do work in Japan do you use a local team to execute the project?

BRUCE MAU: Yes, we do. We hire a firm and contract them. They are the local team but we run the project. So it is slightly different; you are talking about real joint ventures at a very different scale.

Let's see… We have dealt with my questions about structure. But I don't think we have a very coherent or convincing answer to my question about the project. Perhaps we should return to Tom's point about longevity.

THOMAS PAYNE: That is a personal preoccupation of mine, but I believe it reflects the practice because for the most part we are building projects that have to have longevity, especially in the case of institutional clients.

MARIANNE MCKENNA: Not always. Different project types have different life spans. Retail, for example, will be relatively short-lived.

THOMAS PAYNE: There is an ecological side to the issue, too, and it has to do with LEED[10] and sustainability. There is a finite amount of material in the world. Other cultures, European cultures, often look after building fabric better than we have tended to do here in North America where architecture is treated as more disposable. To challenge

this, we've consciously developed attitudes to structure, technique, skin, etc., to create permanence and enduring value in our work as a focus and as a link to sustainability and green architecture. Our vision is that people will be able to, over time, re-inhabit, re-invent, and re-imagine the building. One doesn't get LEED points for that kind of long-range vision, but I think it should count.

BRUCE MAU: In my own practice one of the most satisfying things is simply that people are having families, and the studio is sustaining them. It is really a social function of the business to ensure that people are supported over the long term. One of my primary ambitions is to establish a sustainable long term project where people can find a way to grow inside of the studio without hitting a ceiling.

SHIRLEY BLUMBERG: Which is very hard to do.

BRUCE MAU: Yes, it is quite challenging, so when that happens it is rewarding.

THOMAS PAYNE: I see that as one of our accomplishments. We have tremendous loyalty from people who started with us, and are still here, and it is very gratifying to see how their lives change, and that they stay with us. We have watched their families grow.

MARIANNE MCKENNA: I think having professional partners has been an incredible asset to each of us individually and to the practice. Since we worked together for so many years before starting our own studio we already knew each others' foibles. We did not have to learn them in partnership. Our respective strengths and weaknesses had already been demonstrated. Since then, the practice has gone like this [hand gesture rocking a boat]. It levels off on a regular basis. And different partners take turns at the helm. One of the benefits of a partnership is that when one partner is completely caught up in a project, the others can steer the ship. We also have great support in the financial and administrative network of the office, especially from our comptroller Daphne Harris, and that luxury has allowed us to focus on the work. There are times when the work that you are doing actually sustains more than your share of the practice, and then there are times when you don't have as much work and the converse is true. It is gratifying to see that the boat keeps sailing along…

THOMAS PAYNE: We don't have a managing partner, and we marvel at the way we self-manage, somehow, miraculously. We have strong support … especially from our senior associates Chris Couse and Luigi LaRocca …

MARIANNE MCKENNA: … and good communication …

THOMAS PAYNE: I was saying to the bank manager who looks after our office account today that, at a certain level, we are fiscally conservative in order to be more artistically experimental. We start every week talking about the business side of the practice so that for the rest of the week we can relax and do what we love to do, which is to design, craft and contract architecture.

BRUCE MAU: Okay… let's move on.

There was an article a while ago in *The Globe and Mail* by John Barber, "An architect deconstructs the big 'wow' fad," where he addressed a complaint by a Toronto architect about all the new fancy buildings in Toronto. The argument was that great cities are made out of good, as opposed to great, buildings.[11] Do you remember this article?

BRUCE KUWABARA: No, but it sounds familiar.

BRUCE MAU: When I read it, it felt like arguing that a home should have plumbing but not music when, in fact, a home needs both of these things.

On the other hand, in some of the material that I've read on KPMB you've said that buildings should fit in, not stand out.[12]

MARIANNE MCKENNA: I think we used the word "contextual," inferring that buildings should relate to their context, have a relationship with the fabric … but they should certainly stand out.

THOMAS PAYNE: We would say that there are fabric and object buildings. Sometimes the assignment is to produce more of a figural piece, like Kitchener City Hall or the Stauffer Library, and other times the building wants to be more modestly contextual, like Woodsworth College or King James Place.

BRUCE MAU: It is true, I think, that there is an interesting tension in the work between an obvious sensitivity to context and an ambition to produce an image. The question really is: is one objective getting the upper hand these days?

BRUCE KUWABARA: A lot of our work has involved additions and renovations of existing buildings which draw you into some sort of conversation with what has been there for a longer time. Until now, we haven't done many ground-up, stand alone buildings. But there is always a context. For example, the Concordia University project in Montréal comprises three buildings at the intersection of Ste Catherine Street and Guy Street. At a macro scale, it is infill but there is also an overriding requirement to create an image of the university that will be recognizable on the skyline. But the concept of infill, context and city building is natural to the process of our evolution. We were trained and educated by architects who were always talking about city and

fabric — Barton Myers, George Baird — and, all the while, reading Jane Jacobs. I remember also reading *Ordinariness and Light* by Alison and Peter Smithson.[13] I reveled in that book for the mesmerizing way it captured the radical possibilities of ordinariness, and more subtle spatial experiences in the city.

SHIRLEY BLUMBERG: When I started working with Barton the 45-foot holding bylaw was in effect in the city. It was a tremendously vital time in the development of Toronto — David Crombie was Mayor, and people like John Sewell formed what was considered to be a radical city council. Barton Myers and Jack Diamond played a pivotal role in the preservation of historic neighbourhoods like Yorkville with projects such as York Square, and pioneered the notion of infill housing in Toronto. Crombie's 45-foot bylaw was a temporary measure designed to prevent more developments like St. Jamestown from decimating downtown Toronto.[14] This is the background for our work. These are the events that led to a heightened sense of context and have influenced many of our hybrid projects where historic buildings or fragments of buildings are incorporated into new assemblages.

BRUCE KUWABARA: Our training is in the area of city building but we also believe that every building has its own character and personality. It is not the kind of contextualism where you match everything on the street.

SHIRLEY BLUMBERG: No, but we always take the actual physical context into account. We look at everything around the site for inspiration, but there are always other content-driven issues. Take for example the Festival Centre and Tower for the Toronto International Film Festival Group we are doing across the street from our office at King and John. It is an entire city block. One of the central design challenges is: how does one create a building that expresses film and the idea of the moving image?

THOMAS PAYNE: This loops back to where we started. We talked about how we are different, having a heterogeneous portfolio and not producing a singular *Gestalt* architecture.

So even on a site that is crying out for a strong image, at King and John Streets, we believe the image must somehow resonate with the context. Our work is not about a single commodified expression. I don't think our clients have ever come in with that sort of expectation, whereas some architects, especially solo practitioners of another generation, may encounter it more.

MARIANNE MCKENNA: If you look at this little drawing of the Royal Conservatory of Music (above), you can see the elevation of historic McMaster Hall on Bloor Street and see the Daniel Libeskind crystal right beside it, enveloping the Royal Ontario Museum's historic façade. That is one heck of a neighbour! Right now, there are several prominent commissions by international architects in Toronto — signature, global images that are being dropped into the urban fabric. As architects practising in this city, do we adjust or change our work, our approach, in the face of these projects? It's an open question. I think there will be a push for stronger expression. We have already been influenced. We are not going to start doing singular pieces but the level of dynamic and dramatic image construction in Toronto has and will change the context in which we work.

THOMAS PAYNE: But we are optimistic. We think that collectively these projects speak to the aspiration for greatness in the city.

It is a wonderful moment that we can have a Frank Gehry, a Norman Foster, a Daniel Libeskind and a Will Alsop. To be part of that is a tremendous feeling.

BRUCE MAU: It is fantastic what is going on.

BRUCE KUWABARA: It's exciting for us as a studio, too. We have a lot of new work that is under construction right now that has not been seen or studied. Our work has come in waves. There have been periods of intense construction and then we've had times when we did not have much happening …

Right now we are just coming through a second major construction wave where we have buildings coming up all over the place. And they are different from the ones done during the first period. I always wondered after Kitchener City Hall what the future held in store for us. Would we ever get to do something again of that scope and calibre? Would we ever have the chance to be involved in something that was so public in nature? In my experience, it's a matter of keeping your eyes and mind open and having confidence

that your approach will actually get you there. Eventually another opportunity arises.

At the moment, we have a particular kind of critical urban-focused practice. Yet we are open to the fact that our work may change again.

SHIRLEY BLUMBERG: It is changing, but it has to change in a way that feels authentic to our practice. It's not a matter of suddenly taking a left turn and striving to the status of Libeskind or Gehry. These are unique visionaries whose architecture has achieved a global image. As insiders we feel we are obligated to make our own contribution to the culture of our city, and in a way that contributes to the stature of architecture in Toronto, and Canada in general.

THOMAS PAYNE: We have talked about the different types of practices. Within our practice there are artistic forces, impulses associated with individuals and the team where the art of architecture is foregrounded as a primary and motivating force. Of course, we have a corporate dimension, and this is not to suggest for a minute that one can afford to suspend constant effort and provide the highest level of professional service. We are contracted as professional service providers, not as artists, and often for large dollar amounts. Contemporary building science is a complex, high-stakes affair and must be taken seriously. But if you make the analogy to art, like artists, our challenge is to experiment with certain expressions over time, work through ideas, allow them to become part of the world. Personally, my mind is engaged in the world of composition, form, meaning and texture, not contracts or fees. Yet the two are entwined and we always keep a scientific circuit on top.

BRUCE KUWABARA: I think we have great balance. We are not a small artistic studio, of

which there are many that we could name that are doing extraordinary work, and pushing the limits of every single project. But one of the things about us is that we are able to maintain a productive equilibrium. As we mentioned earlier, we are able to run a project from conception to finish. Our vision of sustainability in our own practice refers not just to the professional fulfillment of the people who work here, but, in a related sense, to the economy of the studio. Our standard is to make enough to give back. We set this out at the beginning. We said we wanted to be in a position to give back, and we've done that.

When we began our practice, we developed an informal strategy that outlined our personal and long range goals and standards, which now has become an essential tool that guides the evolution of our practice. One standard was that the collective attainment of high calibre work would overcome the concern over style, or the question of "what will our work look like?"; and that meant we would never sacrifice the quality of the work. Ever. We would never give in to accepting less.

An early ambition was to set the standards very high so that others in the field would be challenged. Our contribution might be that we raised the bar at a time that it needed to be raised. A lot of younger firms looked at our studio and said, "If they can do it, then so can we, we can be better than them." I think it stimulated people at a moment when there was a kind of lull in the field. The senior figures were all familiar. Everyone else was very small. We rose up quickly, I think in part because there was a vacuum that needed to be filled. But I think our lasting contribution may be that we motivated other firms, specifically practices in Toronto, to be better than they ever would have thought of being themselves.

I think this sort of competitive impulse is a catalyst in various design fields. "If they can do it, let's put ourselves to the test."

THOMAS PAYNE: Part of our project, too, at a kind of pragmatic level and at the level of the opportunity, is to create architecture beyond the borders of Canada. The great thing is that this has now happened. In the States, we've completed the Goodman Theater in Chicago as well as more recent projects for both Yale University — Sprague Hall — and the Trinity College Library in Hartford, Connecticut.

MARIANNE MCKENNA: We've had a new plan in place every three years or so, and on a regular basis we've refreshed the plan. We identified locations where we wanted to do work: in the United States, in Montréal and Ottawa, in Western Canada and in Europe. We also established that we wanted to seek out projects in areas in which we did not have major experience — for instance, science laboratories and medical facilities. One of the things that I believe is that once you've imagined yourself doing something, it is not difficult to make it happen.

BRUCE MAU: Certainly that is my experience. If you've said you *want* to do it, then you *will* do it.

BRUCE KUWABARA: It has been a revelation that we have the capacity and resources to steer our direction and decide our own future.

But what do we want to do next? I think we want to continue to do serious projects that are in the public realm.

I think our strength is in the public realm, meaning publicly funded institutions and buildings — but also private sector projects that engage the public, or address issues of community, culture and socialization. The thing about public buildings is that they are often in the

realm of ideas. The programs and governance of public institutions resonate strongly with our aspirations as a practice.

BRUCE MAU: I noticed that the last book about KPMB (Rockport Publishers, 1997), was organized around the Public and the Private Realms — but you included Sega City @ Playdium and Marc Laurent, which are, respectively, commercial entertainment and retail projects, in the Public Realm.[15]

MARIANNE MCKENNA: That is a broad definition and we do define public very broadly. Perhaps this is naïve but it reflects our commitment to the public realm. If we do a building that is accessible to and nurturing of the public and that might include a retail operation or even a private institution, we think of the building as part of the public realm.

BRUCE MAU: Personally I'm kind of surprised by your cavalier approach to the issue. Perhaps it's because I see in the institutional work a commitment to democratic values that makes a clear distinction between that and private enterprise. I'm all for private enterprise, of course, but I think, in some ways, that the public is under duress at the moment. It's heartening that things are starting to change. In fact, what is happening in our city is an extraordinary new commitment to the public realm that would have been practically unimaginable ten years ago.

But what I'd love to know is: what are the values that inform those projects which are unambiguously "public." For example, when you do a project like a school, or a prison, where is the core sensibility coming from?

MARIANNE MCKENNA: Community… a very strong sense of community…

BRUCE KUWABARA: … a sense of the communal…

SHIRLEY BLUMBERG: … a belief in the public realm…

BRUCE KUWABARA: … and an almost animistic belief in the potential of space to engender and activate culture and community. One of the briefs we were once given asked, "What in your design would encourage interaction?" It was interesting because often clients don't often ask for this level of consideration at the design stage; typically, the issue is seen as one of programming—after the fact. You think about the formation of a building differently when someone asks you a question like that. But the hallmark of our work, I think, would be that we have consistently made public spaces in every single project that we have done. Every single one. Regardless of the size, or type…

MARIANNE MCKENNA: … or whether it was originally in the program or not. We have often, as with the recent building for Genomics and Proteomics Research at McGill University in Montréal, had to eke it out of the program by widening the corridors, making wider staircases with natural lighting at the perimeter of the building so people can hang out in them…. We are constantly arguing for the public realm and trying to squeeze as much social space as possible into a building. If you look at every single one of our projects, you will find a gathering space, very often connected to an exterior space, which gives expression to the building. Without our intervention, the program might simply call for many small rooms, many small labs, linked with circulation. We push to create a heart for each project.

SHIRLEY BLUMBERG: We believe that it is in the interstitial spaces, the spaces between the programmed areas, where the life of the building is really sparked, where the social interaction between people happens most

intensively. At Centennial College we developed a system of light-filled indoor streets, courts and atria that animate the experience of moving through the building, and provide great hang-out space for the students. The design of the college demonstrates our conviction that time spent *between* classes is as important to the learning experience as that spent *in* class.

BRUCE MAU: But you are thinking about the public in terms of social space. A program for a business school is a public project that is about our collective enterprise, but a project like Sega City is about a particular business and their concerns. I think there is a distinction that needs to be made here. For example, we worked on a library in Seattle, and the woman who is the head librarian stated that the library is the cornerstone of democracy. She said that if you were to eliminate the library, democracy itself would become a mockery because an entire class of people would no longer have access to information. So, when you are working in that context, it sets an ambition for the project that is really of the highest order; it is about a high purpose. It is not about the square footage, which you of course have to ultimately resolve, but it is actually about thinking about the future of culture.

So, for me, as we talk here, the answers to the first question begin to emerge — a commitment to longevity as a form of environmental sustainability, community in terms of cultural and social sustainability, and your aspirations of artistic and intellectual engagement with city building and the public realm. These are things that make up the core values of your practice. These values are certainly embodied in a project like a school or a cultural program. But I'd like to hear how democracy is expressed or reclaimed in the context of your work.

MARIANNE MCKENNA: The city halls are probably the strongest examples of that idea of visible democracy…

SHIRLEY BLUMBERG: …or of transparency. It is our instinctive impulse in every project to produce a democratic plan configuration. For example, access to natural light for all offices in our corporate interiors, or a public gathering space which was not in the original program brief. When we redesigned the Council Chamber at Toronto City Hall to accommodate the larger "Megacity" council, ideas about transparent democracy were the subtext of our design. We wanted the design of the chamber to literally reflect our city's democratic process of government. When you think about it at another level, city building is an extraordinary expression of democracy in that you have different architects expressing their voice, their vision all contributing to our collective urban condition.

MARIANNE MCKENNA: There are a number of projects where the retail strategy is to recreate, in a sense, the public realm. Toronto's Eaton Centre is certainly like that—capitalizing on a diagram of urban fabric. It emulates the experience of the interior shopping street, where anyone can go sit on a park bench, and participate in what seems to be a public experience.

Similarly, the design brief for Indigo book stores was positioned more like a project for the public realm—to create an accessible environment where people could go practically 24/7, read anything that was on the shelves, get a cup of coffee, hang out. A meeting place—and what a great spot for a single person! The retail environment began to sound like a reasonable substitute for the community centre or the public library…

BRUCE KUWABARA: …it became a surrogate for the public realm…

MARIANNE MCKENNA: Admittedly, we do operate with a certain naïvete and so we do introduce a lot of the architectural values from our institutional projects, which do represent the public realm, to our private sector clients.

THOMAS PAYNE: What I would like to say is, and I've said this before, and I think it expresses the position of the firm: our objective is to express the values of the client for whom we are working.

SHIRLEY BLUMBERG: We bring a lot of our own values to the work and we hope for a synchronicity and synergy with the client.

BRUCE KUWABARA: But sometimes there are rifts in public opinion. In the case of Toronto City Hall, there was a debate around having public benches in the corridors. We were in favour of them, and I countered with a talk entitled "Imagine a bench-less world." But it was to no avail. What it came down to was security—and crowd control. The irony is that the project was supposed to encourage openness and improve public access.

On the other hand, the Canadian Embassy in Berlin will demonstrate visible democracy—it has a public route through the building, a rare feature for embassy buildings in general, which are usually gated and opaque as a security measure.

MARIANNE MCKENNA: Meanwhile, at Kitchener City Hall, you can see right into the councilors' offices. They accepted a design that would mean they were visible from the public square. The idea was that a citizen could see if a councilor was in, or the mayor was present.

BRUCE KUWABARA: I think there are a lot of things that are in the work that speak to questions of accessibility and transparency in relationship to democracy. Yet I think one has to be very careful about equating transparency with democracy.

Kitchener City Hall was designed so that the councilors' offices are not hidden in the tower, but located on the second floor which is very accessible. The offices have views of the Civic Square and can be seen from the square. The planning of the building reinforces the crossing of paths on a day-to-day basis, so that the movement and visibility of councilors is perceived within the public spaces of the building and site. The intention is to encourage elected representatives to engage the public spaces and their constituents within and around the building.

Accountability is different than transparency.

When we did the renovation of Toronto City Hall it had a seating capacity of approximately three hundred and fifty. In order to increase the accommodation for a larger council of fifty-seven instead of the original twenty-six, we had to take out the first row of public seating.

SHIRLEY BLUMBERG: Yes, we were somewhat conflicted between our responsibilities as architects and our roles as citizens.

BRUCE KUWABARA: It was a clear displacement of citizens.

THOMAS PAYNE: Referring back to the librarian that Bruce Mau mentioned, I think we have been equally fortunate to have enjoyed the leadership of the institutional clients for whom we have worked. The great institutions are often driven by great people who have a tremendous sense of public duty and purpose.

SHIRLEY BLUMBERG: It is wonderful when clients challenge us but then sometimes clients can inspire us by stepping back a bit.

BRUCE MAU: Which brings us to the next question, which relates directly to the subject of the client. I have been very lucky. I've worked with incredible people. But I also know from first-hand experience that in your case you have a kind of generosity and collaborative approach that produces a great deal of commitment on the client's side. Is there a technique to it, or a way of doing it, that you all share?

BRUCE KUWABARA: Well, I think we are both flexible and firm...

MARIANNE MCKENNA: ...and respond to good ideas whatever the source. We know how to roll with the punches...

BRUCE KUWABARA: But ultimately there are standards. We want to reinforce our standards because our vision is as much about the project as it is about the agreement and the relationship with the client.

MARIANNE MCKENNA: We have a tradition of bringing in specialized people to add value to a project. We can be very demanding in our collaborations with our engineering teams. Sometimes we are quite heavy handed, but we also try to inspire them to do their best work with us.

BRUCE KUWABARA: I think a lot of architects have ideals but they don't have standards by which to achieve them. I think Woodsworth College reset the standards across the University of Toronto campus. If you were a historian and were looking into the architectural evolution of the campus, you would see a U of T pre- and post-Woodsworth College. When it was completed in 1991, it was anomalous—a strange and complex hybrid of a building with a courtyard, a cloister...

SHIRLEY BLUMBERG: ...wood windows...

BRUCE KUWABARA: ...and it redefined and kick-started an entire wave of projects which can be traced directly back to Woodsworth in

terms of quality, materiality and the creation of social spaces. It was a perfect example of architectural advocacy initiating a wave of change.

BRUCE MAU: And that was driven by you, Tom?

THOMAS PAYNE: It was a partnership with a couple of key individuals and then the students bought into it. It was the beginning of an appreciation of the importance of part-time education for mature students at the university. Alec Waugh, who was the Vice Principal at the time, always had strong support from the principal and staff and faculty. He went to the students and asked them if they would agree to a self-imposed student levy to ensure that Woodsworth would be equal in calibre to the other more historic colleges which had a tradition of architectural quality. Waugh's efforts were fundamental to the success of the project. At the same time, we were launching our practice so we threw everything we had into it. It was a modest project...

BRUCE KUWABARA: ...but a very influential one... I'd say Woodsworth was one of the most significant projects in the sense we were talking about: raising the standards, changing the direction. Certainly at the University of Toronto they started to rethink architecture.

THOMAS PAYNE: There was a period of ten years where many of the University of Toronto's intellectual leaders became interested in design and its power to improve the environment on campus.

BRUCE MAU: Is your approach in the general relationship with a client to keep them at a distance and present to them at the very end of the design phase? There are two types of client, in my experience. We still meet people who expect

a magical effect. Then there are other people who are interested in the process and like to be really engaged in collaboration.

SHIRLEY BLUMBERG: They want to be in the kitchen...

MARIANNE MCKENNA: ...we really get both types.

BRUCE KUWABARA: Sometimes within the same client group there are people who want to be in the kitchen with you while others prefer to wait for the results.

BRUCE MAU: So your approach is to accommodate both types.

MARIANNE MCKENNA: I think it is much richer when they have input and they understand what is happening. Certainly the best is when they are committed to the work and take ownership. This was really important on the winery project where both Don and Elaine Triggs were fully involved in the evolution of the ideas for the project and then stayed with us through the project's realization. This was such a different type of building experience for all of us. We had their spiritual commitment at each stage along the way.

For the building we just finished at McGill University, the Genomics and Proteomics Research Building, so much of the project had to do with accommodating the program and the approvals process. There was very little discussion about architectural expression. In the end, the client representatives—project managers and physical plant people—were very surprised by how the building turned out. It is contemporary architecture on an historic campus.

THOMAS PAYNE: When we were given the program for Woodsworth College, the client's expectation was that there would be a counter behind an aluminum shutter in the lobby wall

where you could grab a cellophane-wrapped sandwich and a soda. We thought there should be a more celebratory strategy, a big credenza-like element organizing the central common hall with the look and feel of a café or cappuccino bar. It was approved, but the impact of what we were doing did not register. When it was built, they were delighted and the students really used it.

SHIRLEY BLUMBERG: It is about the individual relationship and it is different with every client. Every project has different challenges and you have to figure out ways of communicating with the client that might vary from project to project.

For example, in the case of Centennial College, at one level it was extremely detailed and specific, while at another, it was about the big picture. The ambition of this new building, designed to house the college's high-tech programs, was to create a revitalized identity and image for Centennial that would reposition it within the local academic community.

BRUCE KUWABARA: That is because they did not have a history of great buildings. There was not a lot there at the outset. Concordia is similar. There is an opportunity to bring so much more than they started with. All institutions are not created equally, nor do they operate at the same level.

MARIANNE MCKENNA: Institutions such as Centennial or Concordia don't have the historical longevity or decades of tradition maintained by the University of Toronto or McGill University. Younger universities like Concordia are really inventing themselves. Concordia was a great competition to win. We built on the value that the institution had in the city of Montréal and consolidated a brand for them. We proposed the idea of creating Le Quartier Concordia—a distinctive district comprising the

older buildings and the new one we would build. The fact that the sidewalks of this part of Montréal are, for lack of an alternative, Concordia's green space, takes on new relevance and extends the university's commitment to the improvement of the public realm. There were other big ideas, but this was the main one that really caught their attention.

BRUCE KUWABARA: Right now Concordia is facing student issues about freedom of speech vs. censorship, and all the perennial race issues. Concordia is a battleground, basically. And it's right in the middle of the city.

John van Nostrand[16] once said that "the university is a terrain of conflict." And that is how I think about Concordia. I don't think that about University of Toronto. But describing Concordia as a terrain of conflict seems accurate. In fact, a lot of new universities are combat zones.

MARIANNE MCKENNA: Whereas older universities seem more tamed by tradition, and even if you have an incident at one of the older universities it does not influence the aura of the place the way incidents at the newer universities do.

BRUCE KUWABARA: We come at these issues from different backgrounds and with different priorities. It is interesting, because Tom, I think, is more idealistic, and more committed to things which are time-honoured, which comes out of his experience at Princeton, Yale University and l'École des Beaux-Arts.

BRUCE MAU: And you are not?

BRUCE KUWABARA: I am but in a different way. Once, when Detlef Mertins[17] and I were talking about architecture he said that architecture was an instrument for the production of knowledge. I thought that was an interesting statement.

We had a conversation about new ways of living, new technology, new forms of knowledge. The word "new" was peppered throughout our discussion. I began to wonder whether KPMB was producing anything that approached Detlef's aspirations for contemporary architecture—namely, the pursuit and production of new knowledge.

For Detlef, the project of architecture coincides with the project of modernity, whereas our project of architecture is unwilling to give up the past. It is unwilling to completely turn away from things that are time-honoured. A lot of what we do, you could say, is an innovation of renewal.

SHIRLEY BLUMBERG: It is a reinterpretation of the tradition of architecture.

BRUCE KUWABARA: In a way it is a transformation of ideas.

Some architects are inventive. Others are innovative. There is a difference. I think we are very innovative. Maybe the invention part exists through the sentiment that "all that is old is new again." But I think we are caught in that tension.

BRUCE MAU: If someone said your work is conservative would you be offended?

BRUCE KUWABARA: I don't think so— conservative as opposed to what? What is the opposite? Radical?

MARIANNE MCKENNA: We were once told that we didn't make a short list that we thought we'd get on because…

SHIRLEY BLUMBERG: …we were not edgy enough.

BRUCE KUWABARA: Which makes you go through a lot of introspection.

BRUCE KUWABARA: I think you could say that the work is understated, quiet and polite. You could say that this, in itself, makes it

conservative. But, I believe people form a different impression when they actually come to the work. The work doesn't blare at you, it does not jump at you and say, "Hey, I am a KPMB building!"

SHIRLEY BLUMBERG: Our architecture is about the inhabitation of a building, and how people engage with it. The image does not dominate.

MARIANNE MCKENNA: It is the spatial quality, I think, that moves and surprises people. And it is the connection to the landscape—the relationship between the inside and the outside. In our climate, where we experience many months of winter, the quality of the interior space becomes even more important.

BRUCE KUWABARA: I think our work is digested slowly, over time. It has a slower absorption time, which I think is a good thing. It prohibits us from being constant cover material. But I think it has rewarded us with longevity and staying power.

BRUCE MAU: The architect that this discussion continually reminds me of is Alvaro Siza.

BRUCE KUWABARA: Well, we would be fortunate to be in that realm of comparison.

BRUCE MAU: I've only experienced a few of his buildings but they are almost invisible — except that you immediately notice the beautiful proportions. And then you go and look some more, and you begin to find other things that are extraordinary. For me it is quite exciting, the modesty in the work. That it is not always about — you used the term "cover material" — that it is not always about the image. It is an interesting dilemma for architecture — what the image has to offer, the savagery that it has generated.

BRUCE KUWABARA: Design award programs are often a battle of photography and presentation. Jurors review photographs in binders. Image is everything. A few years ago, I was on a jury for an awards program where there was no time in the schedule to visit the projects, but it turned out after we had signed the awards programs, there was some time to spare. So, with my fellow jurors, we visited the project that we awarded the top prize—which was very good. Then we visited another project which we gave a citation—a Cistercian abbey—and we were blown away. It was a beautiful, primitive, quiet space constructed of load-bearing limestone blocks. It was a clear case in which the photography did not do the work justice.

I think Woodsworth College has a similar problem—because it is a subtle and complex project. To fully appreciate it, you have to experience it directly. The photography has never been able to do it justice because it is not a singular image that can be summarized in one or two shots.

Despite the modesty or silence of some of our own work, we are continually exploring new developments which are affecting the image. One of them is certainly ecological sustainability. We are trying to make buildings that have natural ventilation, or what is called "hybrid ventilation," where you can be in a natural mode, without mechanical equipment, unless it is really cold or hot, in which case you can put on air-conditioning or heat. It is a fascinating proposition because it reconfigures the form of the building. It is also more European in ethos. They have been working on natural ventilation for the last ten or fifteen years. They have thousands and thousands of sustainable buildings. We in North America have a lot of catching up to do …

SHIRLEY BLUMBERG: The incorporation of natural ventilation enabled us to design interior skylit streets with atria for Centennial College. Typically, colleges are built on the high-school model which is a double-loaded corridor building …

BRUCE KUWABARA: … hermetic …

SHIRLEY BLUMBERG: … yes, with the corridors relentlessly lined with lockers and classroom doors. But with Centennial, the criteria for sustainability allowed us to create the atria, which, combined with opening windows in the façade, naturally ventilate the building through the stack effect. This also produces very animated public spaces.

BRUCE KUWABARA: Tom and I are working on a competition for the first new building to be constructed on Parliament Hill in Ottawa since the Confederation Building was completed in the late 1920s. It is the design for the new Senate and the House of Commons. Public Works is running the project, but they have asked for an evaluation of the building in terms of sustainability at the design concept stage, which I think is progressive for Canadian architecture. They feel that this building, post-Kyoto, has to express something that is different and responsible.

MARIANNE MCKENNA: We have been trying to do sustainable buildings for a long time but, more often than not, if there was an additional economic cost involved it would get lopped off. As early as ten years ago our engineers were trying to introduce grey water systems, where you collect rainwater for non-potable use—flushing toilets, watering lawns etc. Where a green idea costs capital, it often gets axed.

BRUCE KUWABARA: You need people who are devoted to sustainable architecture from the beginning.

MARIANNE MCKENNA: We now have a new generation of engineers and clients who are committed to it. For example, on the winery, the client was onside with creating a green building—as long as it didn't cost more. Mark Mitchell, the mechanical engineer, took it on and said, "Okay, I will make it cost less. We will have one chiller for both wine production and air-conditioning, rather than two chillers, and we will minimize dependence on air-conditioning by introducing natural ventilation."

BRUCE KUWABARA: There is a perceptible influence from Europe. There are many contemporary European architects doing work in the United States. In the 1980s, architects like Frank Gehry and Richard Meier were doing work in Europe. For a number of reasons, European architects are now coming to North America. In Toronto, Daniel Libeskind, Will Alsop, Stefan Behnisch and Norman Foster are all doing work. In Ottawa, Dixon Jones is working on the National Portrait Gallery, and there are others.

THOMAS PAYNE: Europe has a sophisticated building technologies industry that produces things that don't exist here.

———

THOMAS PAYNE: There was a recent article on demography in the *New York Times* that stated that in the year 2050 the mean age of a person in the United States will be thirty-six, and in Europe it will be fifty-two and a fraction. What this means is that there will be a declining work force in Europe and that this will have an impact at the global level.

BRUCE KUWABARA: Politically and economically, Europe will diminish in strength. The whole shift will be towards China, India

and the United States and in fifty years from now those countries will still be very strong.

In Europe they are looking at the failure of the pension system because there are no workers to pay into it. It is what we are talking about in Canada except it is happening at a faster, sharper rate in Europe. A lot of people are taking early retirement. They are talking about what a great life it is to be in Vienna in a spa in your fifties. The question is what is the implication of widespread early retirement?

THOMAS PAYNE: The *New York Times* journalist was speculating that to effectively correct the shift you would have to change the retirement rules in Europe and raise the retirement age to eighty.

SHIRLEY BLUMBERG: Currently you have two working people supporting one pensioner. It will be one to one in the year 2050. The only way for them to correct the imbalance is to import about one million immigrants per year…

THOMAS PAYNE: Recently I heard a panel speaker say that the determining factor in terms of the future of the West will be which Western leaders can attract the youngest, brightest people from elsewhere. That will determine our future as much as anything else.

BRUCE MAU: This brings me to my next question. We have covered a lot. There are really two other things that would be interesting to address. One is this notion of social engineering. I thought that the Grand Valley Institution was one of the most interesting projects in the Rockport book. One might call it "new suburbanism."

I have always thought that architecture was a proto-forensic practice. That it is about producing the evidence before the crime is committed. And that, in fact, we are producing a character, a quality of person, when we produce a space.

We know that this is part of the project, but we almost never come out and say it.

SHIRLEY BLUMBERG: There is an expectation of behaviour.

BRUCE MAU: If you make a certain space, you will produce a certain behaviour. For instance, corporate space is devoid of sexuality because nothing is ever supposed to happen there. And that absence — or abstinence — is predicated in the space.

Reading up on Frederick Law Olmstead, as I'm obliged to do at this moment for the competition we won to transform the Downsview military site into a public park for Toronto, you realize he was absolutely unambiguous about his firm's social engineering intentions. They intended to produce a different outcome by designing the space to achieve certain kinds of effects. When you read it, you think, "Whoa, who would say that today?"

MARIANNE MCKENNA: Well, Correctional Services would say something like that. There was a huge ambition for the Grand Valley project. It was rehabilitation vs. punishment. The project brief, called *Creating Choices*, reported on what happened to women when they got out of the Federal penal system after a few years in Kingston's Prison for Women (P4W) in Ontario. These women could not operate on the outside after a lengthy sentence, and the costs to society were enormous. And at that time everyone was sentenced to Kingston regardless of where they were from. There were not enough women in the system— only three hundred and fifty or so — to create regional facilities. There were so many more in the men's system that they could afford to have regional institutions, which meant people could stay in contact with their families. Well, I'm making it sound a little ideal but they

did have the opportunity to stay connected to their community. Whereas, in the case of the women, it didn't matter whether a woman was from the West, or from the Maritimes, or from Quebec, she was placed in P4W. After decades of trying to redress this issue and close down P4W, which was famous as a hell-hole, Correctional Services got approval to create a series of regional, residential communities for women inmates across the country. When we were awarded the commission, we asked them if we could go see other prisons. They said it wasn't necessary. They said, "What we are asking for is a normal residential community like you would find anywhere in Canada." We put forward three models: the university campus, the village green common…

BRUCE KUWABARA: …which was from the Garden City movement and Ebenezer Howard[18] — the idea being that the Garden City was the antidote to the European industrial city. Proponents believed that a village green common could nurture health and well-being, eradicate tuberculosis, promote a healthy family life and a connection to nature…

MARIANNE MCKENNA: …the third model was the resort because they wanted a degree of privacy and seclusion. They chose the village green common model, and we focused on creating a residential community with sidewalks, cottages and porches.

BRUCE KUWABARA: We ended up arguing for porches on the individual cottages. We thought they were an essential response to the issues of community but they were not in the program. The functional program had bedrooms, a living room, a kitchen, but no porch. We allotted 120 square feet per porch. Correctional Services told us that the 120 square feet would have to come out of the budget and that they could not raise additional money for the

porch. So that is what we did.

MARIANNE MCKENNA: Since it was completed in 1996, I have visited to see how it was working, and I saw everything we imagined: a fully operating community of ninety women. The women had carved out their own niches; some were walking around with their carpenter belts, others were planting gardens, and others were cooking. Rather than having meals brought to them, or their clothes washed, the concept was to provide the raw material and equipment and to encourage the women to care for themselves, including the maintenance of their houses and the grounds.

BRUCE KUWABARA: But is it working?

MARIANNE MCKENNA: My impression is that it is working. For example, if a woman is pregnant when she is incarcerated, she is allowed to have her children live with her within the complex up to the age of two-and-a-half years. And I did see babies in strollers. I also saw women using computers in the educational facilities, and women in the workshops learning skills. In a way, it does simulate a community. And this must be good for the women who are inside.

BRUCE KUWABARA: One of the basic yet most interesting ideas was the proposal that the individual beds be allowed to move within a room to express the preference of the resident. In most prisons the bed is bolted to the floor and that's that. The project was about, as the original brief was titled, creating choices. So we tried to build as many opportunities as possible that would allow the women to make choices in their daily life — choices as basic as having windows that open or a bed that can be moved. There was a time when we proposed wood siding for the cottages. Public Works objected, because it would involve maintenance. But our theory was that

maintenance is good; it's part of taking responsibility. The thesis was that you take responsibility for your own environment and therefore your life.

There are so many ways of looking at these projects. Some reinforce the identity of existing institutions, amplifying what they already have. Others replace what they have because it is dated or simply dysfunctional. P4W was the subject of numerous CBC investigative reports calling for its closure.[19] The media attention was stimulated by women's advocacy groups, in particular the Elizabeth Fry Society — a national organization in Canada that campaigns on behalf of women and girls in the criminal justice system. In a way, the project and the issues it raised extended beyond our client.

MARIANNE MCKENNA: Since P4W first opened in 1934, there had been nine attempts to close it down and move it to regional facilities. When we were awarded the contract, they wanted everything completed within twelve months. It took about five years. We went through two attorney generals and two different prime ministers.

BRUCE KUWABARA: And then it won a Governor General's Award, and I'm sure that some people balked. In the end, Grand Valley raised a lot of issues and challenged the values of society: for example, should taxpayers be spending money on a prison rather than on social housing?

MARIANNE MCKENNA: The project was developed during the early 1990s, at a time when the economy was at a high point, so there wasn't much criticism in the beginning. But as the project continued, the economy shifted. Our attitude, right from the start, was to create a facility that would be in sympathy with the women, their issues, their different backgrounds and their situation.

BRUCE MAU: What I've noticed in my collaborations with architects is that they hold the bragging rights to the world's worst business model. Basically every project is a prototype, you assume all the risk, and there is no long term interest in the success of the project. You are as a profession unique in not being able to capitalize on expertise.

And then when someone does come along and develop a more robust model, such as John Portman,[20] for example, he is basically thrown out of the club.

I would be interested in knowing how you deal with that aspect of the business: how do you make it work? Because if you look at the domestic projects you produce, there is no possible way you can be profiting on those…unless I'm mistaken.

BRUCE KUWABARA: We stated when we founded our firm that we wanted to practise architecture at the highest possible level, and profit as well, so that we could give back and have a standard of life that was reasonable. So, that is where we started…

THOMAS PAYNE: The idea that architecture could avail itself of the possibility of multiple reproduction is extremely interesting. If you think of music and musicians, up until the moment that people were able to buy equipment to hear music in the privacy of their homes, workplaces, cars, etc., musicians were getting by on what they could make in live performance. Now the whole music industry has been transformed in terms of the economics. For you [Bruce Mau], there are multiples, and multiple matters. In architecture, if we were trying to capitalize on this phenomenon, one would have to conceptualize a new method. A few months ago I spoke to a developer who was going to do a series of houses that would, at the level of design and detail, be linked

genetically. The concept was that people would be able to build on a portfolio of details and experiment within that envelope. That would be one approach. Another would be to design a building, like an automobile, figuring out a way to produce it over and over again, and making it so well-engineered and designed that people would want it. It takes you back thirty years, to when people were dreaming about industrial housing. There was Renato Severini, but he never did it. He did not get a prototype built but he was envisioning something that would be the follow-up to Habitat.

BRUCE KUWABARA: But the fact is that our practice has successfully sustained itself, with the exception of one year that was not good, that one horrible year…

MARIANNE MCKENNA: But I think Bruce Mau's point is more extensive. It is not just about making money, it is actually about capitalizing on the expertise you have.

BRUCE MAU: Yes, that is the core of the issue. When you look at architecture as a practice, it seems anomalous. It is absolutely committed to the singular when everyone knows that we are as a culture committed to the plural. If automobiles were evolving at the rate that buildings are, they would all still be made of wood.

BRUCE KUWABARA: Except that in a context in which the multiple has replaced the singular, the singular becomes a work of art…

SHIRLEY BLUMBERG: …and the singular becomes highly valued.

BRUCE MAU: If you look at your domestic projects, can you imagine having done any of them with a modular strategy?

BRUCE KUWABARA: Possibly…

MARIANNE MCKENNA: You [Bruce Kuwabara] had that client who came to you and

wanted to create the prototypical modern house in Toronto. He wanted to build one and then roll them out. He had a site in Hog's Hollow, a secluded ravine-like setting in Toronto…

BRUCE KUWABARA: …it was prototypical …that was interesting…

MARIANNE MCKENNA: …but it became personalized. He became obsessed with the idea of a house for himself, and the idea of the roll-out slipped away, and then so did the house itself.

BRUCE KUWABARA: I would like to return to the question: What is really important to us in architecture?

Rob Kastelic, an architect who worked on the Concordia project, said, "I think it is important for architecture to create places for people to loiter." It was a charged statement.

THOMAS PAYNE: Recently, Chris Couse, a senior associate in our firm, and I, went to Montréal with Albert Schultz and Leslie Lester, the artistic director and producing director of the Soulpepper Theatre Company. We visited several of the avant-garde theatre facilities to observe how the lobbies and theatres worked as a complementary whole. We walked through the front door of the Théâtre du Nouveau Monde at midday, and were suddenly in an entirely different world. To our right, there was a veil, and a café behind it; the box office was on the left and conceived as a series of cubic objects within the space, plexi cubes stacked on top with mannequins displaying the costumes of a recent performance. A mezzanine gallery wrapped the space and provided level animation. A thick brick wall at the rear made the feeling of the space even more mysterious. The lobby floor was stepped to follow the city's natural topography, making it more theatrical. We looked into the café and saw a cross section of

the city's population — a couple of young people drinking beer at the bar and an older woman sitting back through the veil to the other side. It was amazing, the architects had engineered a ghost lobby! A unique world. It was a wonderful and casual atmosphere. People were down there, at three o'clock in the afternoon, drinking wine, smoking and socializing...

BRUCE KUWABARA: ... like in Paris. All the architects there work very hard, but when they reach a certain point in the day they stop. And they just go off and have a great meal with a great wine. I talked to Alan Levitt, a colleague who practises in Paris, and he said that is the way they live. They think we North Americans are nuts, that we work too much.

THOMAS PAYNE: At l'École des Beaux-Arts, where I studied for one year, they locked the door at eight o'clock in the evening. If you stayed inside you were there for the whole night. The concierge would come and lock the doors. Before the *charrette*, we'd put money on the table, and some designated students would go out and get a shopping wagon and load it with wine, beer, salami, cheese and bread. Everyone would be drinking (but the helpers would consume more alcohol than those seeking credits). People would stagger out in the morning...

BRUCE KUWABARA: The biggest trick in this profession, because it is hectic, is to try to have as much fun as possible.

Your earlier question [Bruce Mau] was: are you conservative? I think it is more that we are thorough. We are extremely rigorous and detail-oriented.

BRUCE MAU: To get people to actually make that level of commitment to the values and the standards of your practice says something.

BRUCE KUWABARA: We are better balanced now. There were times when the sheer amount of work, the hours, the results and the pay were not combining to make a great formula. But we changed that.

THOMAS PAYNE: It does say something. And it should weigh heavily on your mind when you are designing a project worth millions of dollars. It could be the most expensive thing the client has ever done, and if it doesn't work out, it could be costly at an economic, emotional and psychological level. The profession of architecture is so deadly serious that you have to have fun with everything you do, every day.

BRUCE KUWABARA: And I do!

THOMAS PAYNE: Yet that doesn't alter the fact that we have serious responsibilities.

BRUCE MAU: We are about to wrap up our conversation. Let's return once more to the question of the studio and your ideals. I once read this incredible discussion between Peter Eisenman and Frank Gehry. At some point in the discussion Peter asked Frank, "Why don't you make it easier? Why don't you do things that are rectilinear? Why do you make everything so difficult? If you made it simpler, and did the postmodernist thing, then everyone would understand it and build it easily." Frank said, "I would do that if I could, but I couldn't bear to go home and tell my children that I don't have a way of responding to the issues of my time. That I don't have my own ideas about this moment in history." I thought that was an incredible way of framing a practice.

So my final question to you is this: is the studio a model for a way of living, and if it is, how does that manifest itself?

MARIANNE MCKENNA: In a way it is, in that our relationships and the evolution as a practice parallels what is going on in our society. We believe in creating a community

component for every project, and we take opportunities to better define the relationships between people's living and working environments.

BRUCE KUWABARA: Our model is very collegial. What does that mean? It means peers; an interplay of respect and openness. Of course, there are occasional disagreements.

THOMAS PAYNE: But we prioritize and make creativity and the artistic output the prime focus. Although we are concerned about the economic performance of the individual projects, only rarely is there ranting and raving about internal financial targets.

SHIRLEY BLUMBERG: Our studio stems from the belief that the different talents and abilities create stronger work.

MARIANNE MCKENNA: We have forged our own model. There is no directly comparable model.

BRUCE KUWABARA: There are a couple — such as Hariri and Hariri, but they are sisters.

MARIANNE MCKENNA: But there is no model where there are two female and two male partners who are not somehow related or involved.

THOMAS PAYNE: Anyway, we've been practicing in our building together for a long time ... almost twenty-five years ... from the time we worked with Barton ...

I can't believe that it was almost twenty-five years ago we started working together ...

Notes

1. From Sarah Milroy, "The mural that rocked Canada," *Globe and Mail*, 2 June 2003. Milroy uses the term in reference to Vancouver artist Brian Jungen: "Brian Jungen's Nike sneaker sculptures, mask-like forms made by dissecting consumer products mass-produced in Asia, [are] uneasy and complex hybrids, not unlike the country itself."

2. Barton Myers Associates was founded in Toronto in 1975 as a full-service architecture and planning firm. In 1984, Barton Myers opened an office in Los Angeles, where he began to teach at the UCLA Graduate School for Architecture and Urban Planning. He moved there permanently in 1987. His four Toronto associates chose to stay in Toronto, in the same King Street building, and formed KPMB Architects.

3. John Ralston Saul, *Reflections of a Siamese Twin: Canada at the End of the Twentieth Century* (Toronto: Penguin/Viking, 1997).

4. *Ibid.* Saul's central point is that while all cultures are complex, the central characteristic of Canadian culture is its complexity; that although Canada has a tripartite foundation it does not exclude other individuals or ethnic groups.

5. George Baird is a partner in the Toronto-based architecture and urban design firm Baird Sampson Neuert Architects Inc., Professor of Architecture at the Harvard University Graduate School of Design and Dean of the Faculty of Architecture, Landscape and Design at the University of Toronto. Baird's recent academic research has focused on the social and political aspects of the design of public space, and on that of housing constructed in existing medium-density residential neighbourhoods. Both Bruce Kuwabara and Thomas Payne worked for George Baird before joining Barton Myers Associates; Baird was also Shirley Blumberg's thesis advisor at the University of Toronto.

6. Grand Valley Institution for Women, Kitchener, Ontario, completed in 1996, was the first of five new regional residential facilities designed to house federally-sentenced women. The regional facilities were intended to replace the seriously outmoded Prison for Women (P4W), built in Kingston, Ontario in 1909. An innovative program for the new facilities, based on the idea of rehabilitation rather than punishment, was outlined in a taskforce document called *Creating Choices*. This document served as a basis for the project.

7. Bill Buxton is a designer and a researcher concerned with human aspects of technology. His work reflects a particular interest in the use of technology to support creative activities such as design, filmmaking and music. Buxton is currently Principal of his own boutique design and consulting firm, Buxton Design. From 1994 until December 2002, he was Chief Scientist of Alias/Wavefront, a high-tech research and development company based in downtown Toronto (see note 9). He is also an Associate Professor in the Department of Computer Science at the University of Toronto.

8. Patricia Ward Biederman and Warren G. Bennis, *Organizing Genius: The Secrets of Creative Collaboration* (Boston: Addison Wesley, 1997). In the book, University of Southern California business professor Bennis and Los Angeles Times reporter Biederman examine six "Great Groups" whose work affected and sometimes changed the modern world.

9. KPMB transformed six floors of four interconnected historic warehouse buildings in downtown Toronto into 100,000 square feet of studios and offices for Alias/Wavefront — a high-tech research and development company with an international reputation for producing cutting-edge entertainment and design software, including the Academy Award winning software Maya. The building was completed in October 1997.

10. The LEED (Leadership in Energy and Environmental Design) Green Building Rating System is a voluntary, consensus-based American standard for developing high-performance, sustainable buildings. Members of the U.S. Green Building Council representing all segments of the building industry developed LEED to establish a common standard, promote integrated design practices, encourage environmental leadership in the building industry, raise consumer awareness of green building benefits and transform the building market.

11. John Barber, "An architect deconstructs the big 'wow' fad," *Globe and Mail*, 14 May 2002. In the article, Barber addresses statements made by outspoken architect Michael Kirkland who in a public lecture at the Toronto City Archives denounced the "half a billion dollars" spent on "architectural megastatements at the Art Gallery of Ontario and the Royal Ontario Museum," and dismissed Toronto's "new infatuation with avant-garde architecture as a crass marketing campaign." Barber concurs, "It's

always hard to find people sufficiently nasty to tell the truth, and his stinging denunciation of 'a wretched excess of world-class follies' had the ring of it." But Barber concludes on an open note, "Is it certain that Toronto's latest bids for architectural prominence will flop? I don't know. Perhaps the great risks of the wow strategy will pay commensurate benefits."

12. Bruce Mau is referring to a statement made by Larry Richards, Dean of the Faculty of Architecture, Landscape and Design at the University of Toronto in "KPMB: It is what it is," by Mark O'Neill in *Nuvo*, Vol. 4, no. 2 (Summer 2001): 56–62. Larry Richards was quoted as saying: "Munk [Munk Centre for International Studies at U of T] represents for KPMB the idea that buildings should be part of a larger idea about the campus, they should fit in rather than stand out. They've taken the side of the master plan that says buildings should bring more coherence to the university as a whole."

13. Alison and Peter Smithson, *Ordinariness and Light: Urban Theories 1952–60* (Cambridge: M.I.T. Press, 1970). Peter Smithson (d. 2003 at age 79) was one of the most influential figures in post-war British architecture. With his wife and architectural partner Alison, Smithson was an early proponent of what the critic Reyner Banham termed the "New Brutalism," importing modernist trends from mainland Europe and America while maintaining a distinctly British approach. Their work — notably The Bath University School of Architecture, completed in the 1980s — was criticized by some for being uninteresting, though this was arguably intended. Ordinariness was an idea they explored throughout their oeuvre.

14. In the early 1970s, Mayor David Crombie enacted a 45-foot height bylaw — in an effort to stall further development. The bylaw provided the City of Toronto with several years (the length of Crombie's term in office, 1972–1978), in which to strategically reconsider the development of its downtown.

15. Lucas H. Guerra, ed., *Kuwabara Payne McKenna Blumberg* (Gloucester, Mass.: Rockport Publishers, 1997). The book is part of Rockport's *Contemporary World Architects* series. KPMB is the only Canadian firm included in the series.

16. John van Nostrand is a partner with the Toronto firm architectsAlliance. He is an Adjunct Professor at the Faculty of Architecture, Landscape and Design, University of Toronto. He writes and lectures extensively on subjects as varied as Canadian

urban history, waterfront revitalization, and community development in the Third World.

17. Detlef Mertins, former Associate Professor at the Faculty of Architecture, Landscape and Design, University of Toronto, and now Chair of the Department of Architecture at University of Pennsylvania, is an architect, historian, and critic. See his essay, "Toronto Style," in this book.

18. Sir Ebenezer Howard (1850–1928) was an English town planner and principal founder of the English garden-city movement. His book *Tomorrow: a Peaceful Path to Real Reform* (1898), reissued as *Garden Cities of Tomorrow* (1902), outlined a model self-sustaining town that would combine town conveniences and industries with the advantages of an agricultural location.

19. The Canadian Broadcasting Corporation (CBC) is Canada's national public broadcaster. On April 26, 1994 the Institutional Emergency Response Team (IERT), an all-male team of guards, was called into Kingston's P4W, Prison for Women, after the warden declared a state of lockdown. The videotape showed women prisoners being strip-searched and brutally treated by the male guards. This incident was brought to light through the CBC's *Fifth Estate* story entitled "The Ultimate Response." The events which occurred at the P4W created concern among the Canadian Human Rights Commission, Amnesty International and Penal Reform International. As a result of the incident in Kingston, the Task Force on Federally Sentenced Women took effective action with their document *Creating Choices*, which recommended opening five regional facilities (see note 6) as well as a unique healing lodge for Aboriginal women. This approach emphasized self-sufficiency and the ability of federally sentenced women to live in dignity and respect. As a result of these initiatives, P4W was officially closed in 2000.

20. John Portman & Associates is best known for introducing the modern atrium to corporate design. From its inception in 1953, the firm has concentrated on the "practical development" of urban architecture, community revitalization and suburban mixed-use projects.

PAGES 22–41: Photo essay by Maris Mezulis, 2003, showing KPMB partners in conversation with Bruce Mau (pp. 22-23), Ravine House (pp. 24-25), Kitchener City Hall (pp. 26-27), Tudhope Associates (pp. 28-29), Woodsworth College (pp. 30-31), Jackson-Triggs Niagara Estate Winery (pp. 32-35), King James Place (pp. 36-37), Joseph S. Stauffer Library at Queen's University (pp. 38-39), Richmond City Hall (pp. 40-41).

Selected Work

1987–2004

The First Three Projects

1987–1989 TORONTO

In its first few years of practice, KPMB was awarded two competitions for large-scale institutional projects: Kitchener City Hall and
the Joseph S. Stauffer Library at Queen's University. KPMB also
continued to work in association with Barton Myers to complete the
renovations and additions to Woodsworth College at the University
of Toronto. While these projects were being realized, the practise
simultaneously focused on the design and construction of smaller-
scale interior intervention projects that could be completed in
shorter time frames. This early work established the firm's design
and production standards, and laid the foundation for an architectural language that would inform the larger-scale institutional
and commercial projects.

Marc Laurent 1986–1989: The first project began as a collaboration between the owner, Henry Bendayan, and Bruce Kuwabara
and Thomas Payne, and involved two phases of refurbishment of an
existing retail shop located on Bloor Street West, Toronto's high-
end retail street. The collaboration continued with additional phases
completed in 1991 and 1994. The design is characterized by curved
planes inflected off rectilinear floor and ceiling grids; overlapping
screens and suspended canopies; and the juxtaposition of industrial materials — such as prefinished steel, polished aluminum and
rubber — with natural materials such as flamed granite and bird's
eye maple veneer.

Dome Productions at the Skydome 1989: A subsidiary of The
Sports Network (Canada's all-sports television channel), this project
was one of the first facilities of its kind to integrate live-event
broadcasting and post-production editing. Sandblasted glass and
aluminum screens at 40-foot intervals amplify the segmented,
radiating order of the SkyDome's concrete structure and define
curving spines of movement along both floors. A granite-topped
cappuccino bar is integrated with one of the staircases, and corridors function as spaces for both circulation and social gathering.

Tudhope Studios 1989: The studios for this marketing and communications firm involved the renovation and upgrade of a 1940s
warehouse building. Two large-scale stucco panels recompose the
original façade, while retaining its legibility. Aluminum mullions and
sills re-proportion the existing windows, a compositional device
that was later adapted in the treatment of windows on the Civic Walls
of Kitchener City Hall. Inside, a series of steel and perforated metal
screens define workstations, meeting areas and circulation systems.

TOP: Marc Laurent.

MIDDLE: Dome Productions at the Skydome.

BOTTOM: Tudhope Studios.

Woodsworth College, University of Toronto

1991 TORONTO

The University of Toronto's historic downtown campus may be characterized as a series of individual colleges. The vision was to bring
Woodsworth, the most recent college on campus, to a position of parity
with the other colleges. This was achieved by emphasizing permanence and enduring value in the quality of materials and craftsman-
ship. The university community's strong commitment to extending and
enhancing the college's facilities inspired generous funding, including
a self-imposed student levy accounting for more than half of the total
construction cost. Woodsworth was also one of the transitional projects marking the emergence of the practice from Barton Myers, and is
one of the seminal projects of KPMB.

The project required the renovation of three existing buildings for
administrative and faculty offices and new additions for classroom
and student gathering spaces. Conceived as an exercise in urban infill
and adaptive re-use, it resulted in the re-interpretation of the academic quadrangle. A two-storey L-shaped masonry building extends
the surrounding typology of low brick buildings and unites three dis-
parate heritage structures — a Victorian residence (1891), and the ROTC
Drill Hall and Officer's Quarters (1939–1941) — into a cohesive urban
complex which encompasses a green courtyard bordered by a ground-
level cloister lined with glazed-wood operable doors. The street façade
is deliberately reticent to respond to the heritage context, limited to
a brick entry tower and two brick and stone gateways which link the
existing Victorian houses. Inside, a material palette of red brick, limestone, Quebec granite and teakwood articulates a series of hallways
and public spaces to weave existing and new parts together. Classrooms
are furnished with custom desks and slate blackboards. The space
between the Drill Hall and the Victorian houses is conceived as a
social gathering room in the spirit of the traditional Great Hall, with
its large brick fireplace and communal bar.

The result offers a contemporary reinterpretation of traditional
collegiate architecture, inherent in the communal spaces of circulation
and gathering (which formally recall the quadrangle, cloister and great
hall), in the emphasis on material authenticity and in the attentive
crafting of stone, wood and steel details throughout.

Woodsworth College was completed as an association of Barton Myers Architect
Inc. and Kuwabara Payne McKenna Blumberg Architects.

ABOVE: The quadrangle.

RIGHT: Gateway linking Victorian houses.

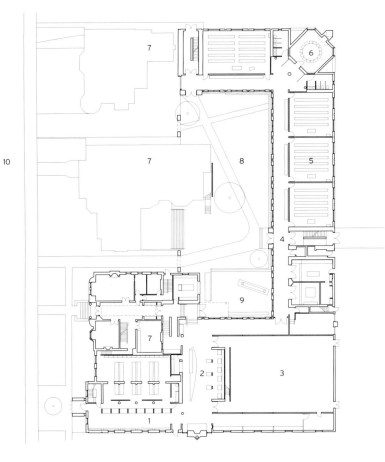

Ground floor

1   foyer/registration
2   café/bar and student lounge
3   Drill Hall
4   cloister
5   classroom
6   seminar room
7   Victorian house
8   outdoor quadrangle
9   terrace and fountain
10 St. George Street
11 administrative office

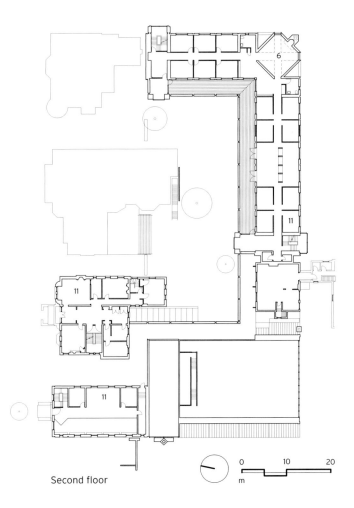

Second floor

0   10   20
m

Public spaces and circulation routes are woven through and between existing and new buildings.

RIGHT: The corridor between the café/bar and Victorian houses.

OPPOSITE, TOP: The café/bar and student lounge.

OPPOSITE, BOTTOM RIGHT: A convertible cloister provides access to the quadrangle and classrooms.

Reisman-Jenkinson Residence

1991 RICHMOND HILL, ONTARIO

This private residence and studio located in Richmond Hill, a suburb
north of Toronto, represents the studio's first domestic project and
demonstrates a belief in the dialectical relationship of life and architecture. Designed for a sculptor and a writer and their two children, the
house challenges the conventions and cultural limitations associated
with suburban life. The program of flexible living and work spaces was
conceived to accommodate the rituals of family and domestic life,
as well as to host artistic events, musical performances and a private
Hebrew school.

The building is organized as four individual but linked structures of
light-grey, split-faced concrete block which together define a forecourt
and inner courtyard and conserve a stand of existing silver maple trees.
With its shaped roof and clerestory windows, the volume in the forecourt displaces the conventional garage location with a sculpture studio.
A glazed entrance "porch" appears to be slipped in between the studio
and the main living space and defines the south edge of the forecourt.
Bedrooms and writing studios are located deep in the plan and grouped
around the inner garden court. High ceilings, large door and window
openings and maple hardwood floors engender a loft-like atmosphere
while sliding panels in the transitional spaces between the buildings
allow spatial transformation for degrees of openness and privacy.

ABOVE: Forecourt showing glazed entrance porch
and sculpture studio with shaped roof, fabricated
from anodized, preformed aluminum panels.

51

ABOVE: Main living space with fireplace fabricated
in oil-finished sheet steel.

OPPOSITE: The glazed volume of the front entrance
porch separates the central living and kitchen zone
from the sculpture studio.

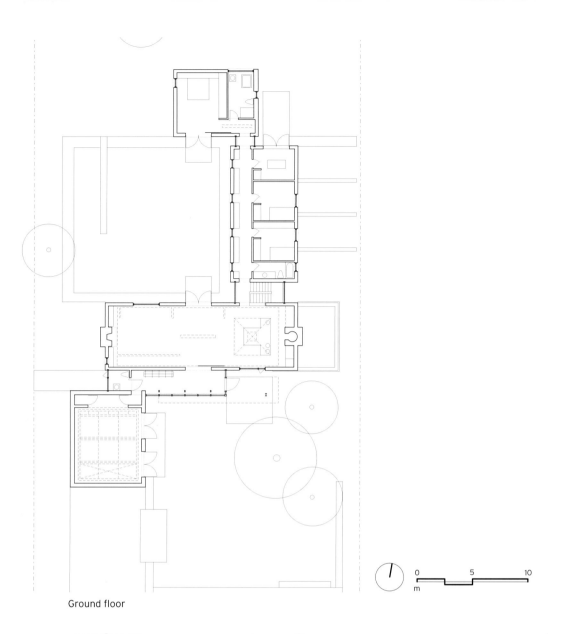

Ground floor

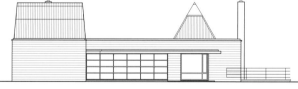

South elevation

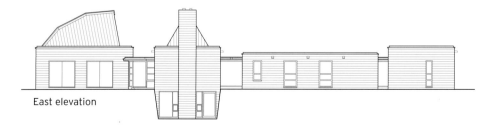

East elevation

OPPOSITE, TOP: A continuous plane of maple hardwood flooring contrasts exposed split-faced concrete block walls.

OPPOSITE, BOTTOM: Furniture is custom-made millwork faced with maple veneer. An aluminum screen divides the wood stair leading to the basement.

King James Place

1991 TORONTO

King James Place houses the Canadian headquarters of the British advertising agency Saatchi and Saatchi. As one of KPMB's earliest urban infill projects, it was also one of the first buildings in Toronto to respond to stringent guidelines for the construction of new architecture in historic urban contexts.

Sited on King Street East, the historic centre of the city and one of the main commercial streets of nineteenth-century Toronto, the building completes a significant city block by filling in two empty sites between St. Lawrence Town Hall (1849) and the York Belting Building (1888). It faces St. James Anglican Cathedral (1850) and a Victorian garden park across the street. Also in compliance with city guidelines, the reconstructed façade of a heritage warehouse building is incorporated into the elevation — where it is assigned a central position.

The new building establishes alignments, registrations and material and tectonic relationships with the adjacent buildings. The predominantly limestone and brick structure stands five storeys but is terraced back at the upper two levels to reduce the impact of its massing and to appear as a three-storey building, preserving an important view of the St. Lawrence Hall cupola to the west. The height and cornice lines are aligned with those of the adjacent historic buildings. The north-facing exterior is divided into a rhythm of paired bays, resonant with the double-bay façade of the York Belting Building to its west. An octagon anchors the complex on the south-east and formally turns the corner of the building into Market Square, a pedestrian route that links King Street to Front Street.

The building concept rejects the need to make a singular statement in favour of a cooperative response to its context. While it does acquiesce to a group existence, a distinctive presence nevertheless emerges at the scale of the pedestrian experience, where the complexity of the façade's depth and texture is revealed in the detailing of the window mullions and channel reveals, and in the precision of the metal and masonry work.

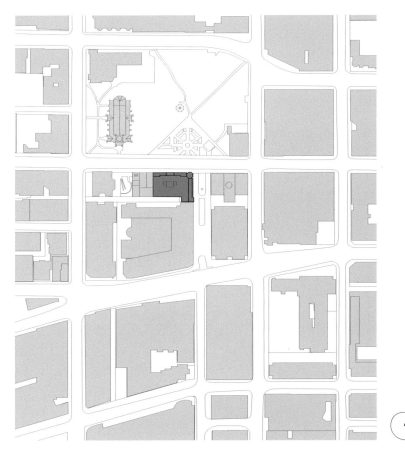

1

Kitchener City Hall

1993 KITCHENER, ONTARIO

The City of Kitchener, formerly named Berlin because of its early settlement by German immigrants, is the largest city within the region of Waterloo in south-western Ontario. It is also renowned for hosting North America's largest annual Bavarian Festival, "Oktoberfest." In 1973, the Beaux-Arts-style City Hall and Farmer's Market (1925) were demolished in favour of a new "Market Square" shopping centre. This action diminished the image of the downtown and created a sense of civic loss. The city soon reconsidered its urban development goals, and in 1988 launched a national design competition for a new city hall that would give momentum to its improved revitalization strategy. KPMB's scheme was selected from 153 submissions.

The design responds to the goals of the competition brief, which was developed under the direction of Detlef Mertins, the Professional Advisor of the competition. Invoking classic civic precedents such as the agora, amphitheatre and plaza, the overall program is resolved by a U-shaped configuration consisting of two Civic Wall buildings which encompass the resultant Civic Square and Tower. Both front onto King Street, the city's main street. The Civic Wall buildings define the perimeter of the site and express the change of topography from three storeys at King Street to two storeys at Duke Street. Within these walls, the Council Chamber — a metal clad volume with a curved roofline, and the Administrative Offices, articulated as tower, wall and slab — flank the centrally placed void of the Civic Rotunda to form an ensemble of balanced asymmetry. With its double height and directional steel truss roof surrounded by clerestory windows, the Rotunda creates a concave indoor gathering space for public use. The top of the Civic Tower is composed as a modular cube and functions as a weather beacon.

The architectural concept posits the idea of the building as both figure and ground, recomposing itself as it is experienced. At street level, the Civic Walls, clad in red sandstone and articulated by a serial repetition of windows, are modulated to the materials and proportions of red brick buildings that distinguish the heritage fabric of Kitchener. In juxtaposition, the monumental, distinctive forms of the Civic Rotunda and the Tower stand out as visible landmarks of the city.

The project demonstrates visible democracy in its composition of accessible internal and external spaces that remain penetrable beyond normal civic business hours. Specifically, the diagonal pedestrian path that cuts through and passes by the circular form of the Rotunda was strongly influenced by James Stirling's plan for the Neue Staatsgalerie Stuttgart (1977).

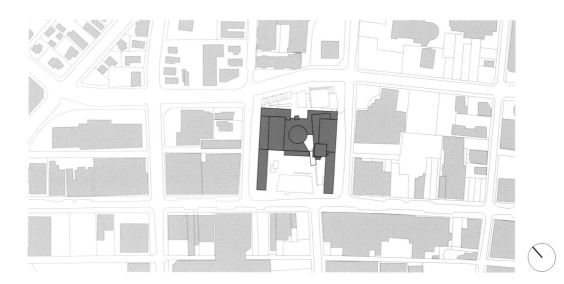

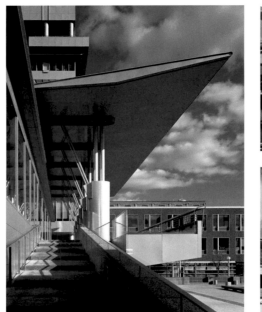

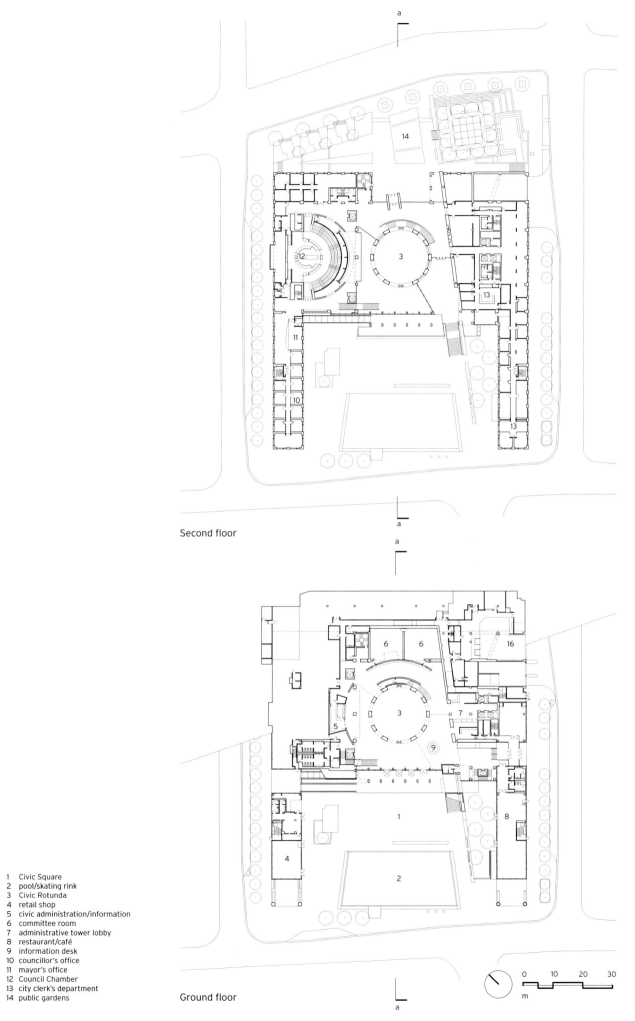

Second floor

1 Civic Square
2 pool/skating rink
3 Civic Rotunda
4 retail shop
5 civic administration/information
6 committee room
7 administrative tower lobby
8 restaurant/café
9 information desk
10 councillor's office
11 mayor's office
12 Council Chamber
13 city clerk's department
14 public gardens

Ground floor

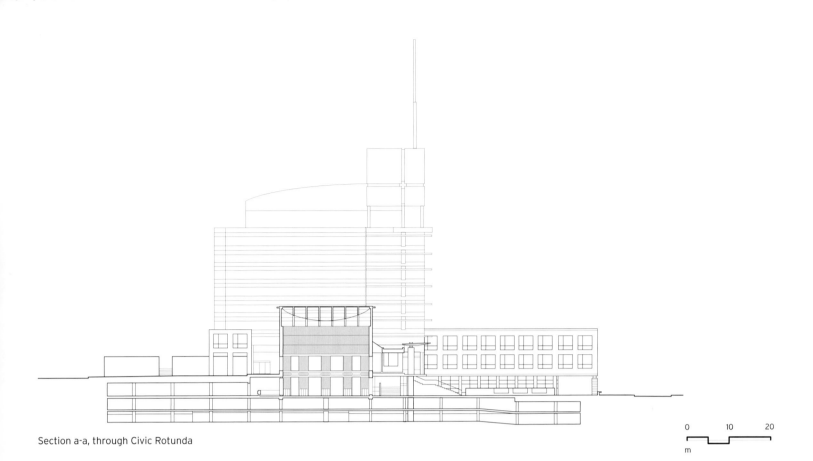

Section a-a, through Civic Rotunda

RIGHT: The volume of the Council Chamber intersects the second floor foyer, which overlooks the Civic Rotunda beyond.

OPPOSITE: The interior of the stone-clad Civic Rotunda is lined with oak strips.

Design Exchange

1994 TORONTO

The Design Exchange (DX) is North America's first comprehensive design centre. A not-for-profit institution, its mandate is to promote the economic and cultural importance of design. Located in the heart of Toronto's financial district, the new institution occupies the heritage Art Deco Toronto Stock Exchange (c. 1937) and the first four floors of the Ernst and Young Tower, part of the expansion of Mies van der Rohe's Toronto Dominion (TD) Centre (1963–68).

The 40,000-square foot project transforms and clarifies the existing layout of heritage and contemporary structures to accommodate a program which includes exhibition space, a multi-purpose hall, a resource centre, a members' lounge, seminar rooms, as well as a café and a retail store. The public route through the building moves between the internalized spaces of the Art Deco building and the contemporary spaces of the office tower. The public image of the Design Exchange is defined by a system of interventions — walls, ceiling planes and stairs — distinct from the existing structures.

The historic Trading Floor of the former Stock Exchange forms the heart of the project and was restored as a multi-purpose space with retractable auditorium seating and a new bridge/stair. The bridge/stair links the Trading Floor to the north and south wings of the third-level office building and creates a platform from which to view the restored Charles Comfort murals. The platform steel structure is finished in the same graphite paint specified by Mies van der Rohe for the exterior treatment of the steel towers of the TD Centre.

On the third level, a meeting room, exhibition hall and two-storey resource centre lock into the Miesian grid of the office tower. The resource centre, overlooking Mies' banking hall and the plaza, is a long and narrow two-storey space with bookshelves mounted on an internal structural wall with an integral catwalk providing access to upper shelving.

Stone, sandblasted glass and stainless steel for the new elements reference and complement both heritage and contemporary structures. The colour scheme of chartreuse, ochre and azure was derived from the Charles Comfort murals and is strategically woven through the historic and new spaces of the institution.

Section a-a, through Trading Floor
and resource centre

0   5   10

m

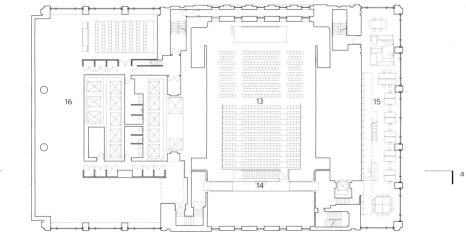

Fourth floor

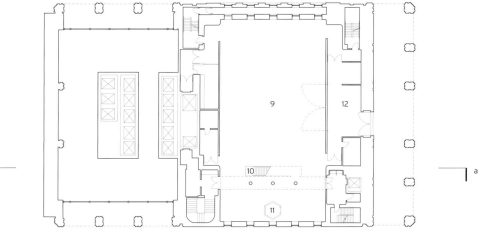

Trading Floor and third floor

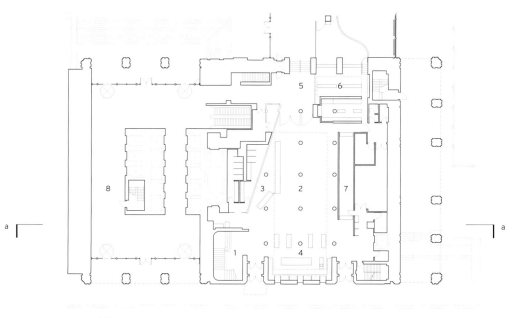

Ground floor

1 historic lobby entrance
2 exhibit area
3 reception
4 retail
5 concourse entry
6 café
7 cloak room
8 Ernst Young tower lobby
9 historic Trading Floor
10 stair/bridge
11 historic Trading Booth
12 seating and exhibition storage
13 Trading Floor with
   retractable seating
14 bridge
15 resource centre
16 exhibition gallery

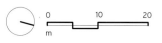

TOP ROW: Information desk and retail at ground floor.

MIDDLE ROW: Detail of stair leading to catwalk and two-storey resource centre.

BOTTOM ROW: Views of third floor exhibition space.

Joseph S. Stauffer Library, Queen's University

1994 KINGSTON, ONTARIO

The Joseph S. Stauffer Library at Queen's University is situated in Kingston, a former British garrison town and the historic capital of Upper Canada on the north-eastern shore of Lake Ontario. The project was the winning scheme in a national design competition to create a new research library for the humanities and social sciences and to implement the University's vision to create a library for the twenty-first century.

The library occupies the north-west corner of the principal campus intersection. Conceptually, the plan inverts the normative order of the traditional college quadrangle to the street. The form is conceived as an assemblage of perimeter elements around a central edifice — a light-filled, three-storey atrium that organizes the plan. The perimeter elements are scaled to relate to the neighbouring buildings and contain reading and study rooms. An octagonal stone and glass element marks the main entrance, and stands out in the otherwise orthogonal building fabric. Inside, a suspended helical staircase divides the north-south circulation spine into separate atria, and injects a dynamic element within the iterative plan order of stacks and reading rooms.

The tectonics of structural framing are a central theme in the architectural expression; concrete elements are left exposed to clarify its reading. The structural modules encompass the stack modules, the arrangement of which exceeded conventional requirements to allow wider aisles for wheelchair access.

The project represents a contemporary translation of Collegiate Gothic architecture. In expression and materiality, it references the vertical proportions, variegated silhouettes and material authenticity of academic architecture at Queen's, as well as precedents such as King's College Chapel at Cambridge and All Souls College at Oxford. Masonry, wood window frames and metal roofing resonate with the heritage campus fabric while fabricated metal components, an aluminum curtainwall and skylight systems anchor the contemporary image of the building. Traditional forms and materials are translated into a modern idiom with present day methods and systems. To achieve material authenticity within budget limitations, local conventions of limestone construction were re-interpreted as a unit stone masonry veneer system, with machine-split limestone blocks laid up in traditional ashlar. Piers and chimneys are topped with aluminum finials incised into the stone cladding to produce a cumulative vertical expression.

The library was completed by KPMB in association with Moffat Kinoshita Architects.

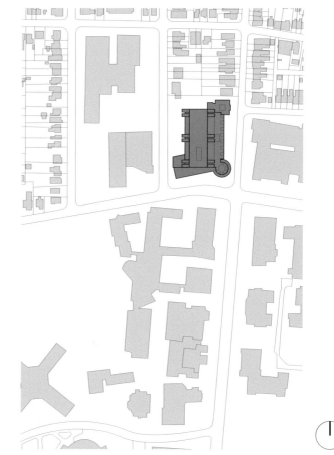

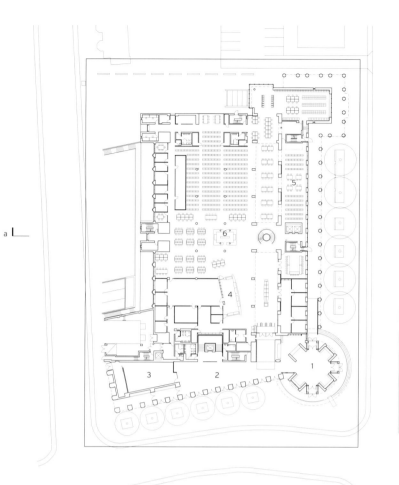

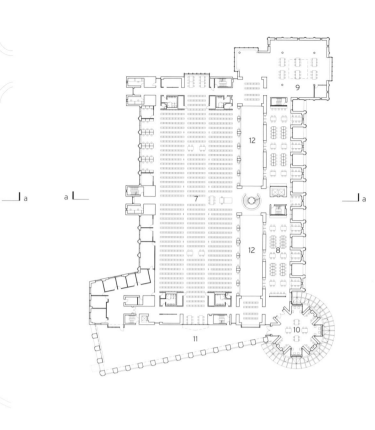

Ground floor

1 entrance
2 lobby/café
3 art gallery
4 circulation
5 current periodicals
6 information/reference
7 stacks
8 garden reading room
9 graduate reading room
10 fireplace reading room
11 sculpture terrace
12 open to below

Second floor

0 10 20 30
m

OPPOSITE: The alcove in the fireplace reading room is finished in cherrywood-paneled walls and custom millwork.

Joseph S. Stauffer Library, Queen's University

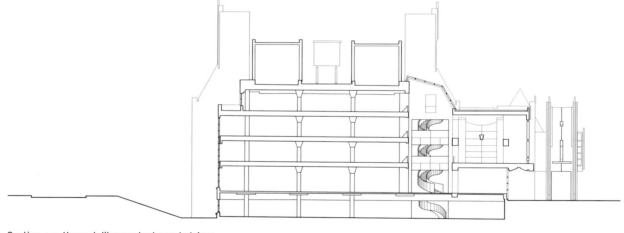

Section a-a, through library stacks and atrium

0   5   10   15
m

ABOVE: Suspended helical stair with cherrywood
balustrade.

Grand Valley Institution for Women

1996 KITCHENER-WATERLOO, ONTARIO

The program for the Grand Valley Institution for Women emphasizes the reintegration into society of women serving federal sentences. The project responded to the 1990 Canadian government report *Creating Choices*, which was implemented by Correctional Services Canada and propelled by women's advocacy groups. It was the first of five regional centres built to replace the notorious central Prison for Women (P4W) in Kingston, Ontario. The architectural challenge was to translate the report's recommendations into built form, and to replace the institutional atmosphere of women's prisons with a residential environment. The community of Kitchener-Waterloo, with its local industry and network of post-secondary education, was selected for its potential to offer a supportive context for work and study outreach programs.

The plan derives from the village model, with buildings organized around a shared central green, and involves a concept of layering, from public spaces for community gathering to private spaces for individual retreat and reflection. The institutional character of the main building is modified by the articulation of the program elements — administration, visiting areas and training rooms — into a series of low volumes interconnected by a loggia with generous windows facing the green. A non-denominational, ecumenical space of worship and healing, expressed as a cylindrical form, occupies a pivotal position in the plan and displaces the traditional role of the surveillance tower.

The complex is internalized to ensure security and privacy as well as to respect local community perceptions. Façades exposed to public view are intentionally modest and discreet, with limited door and window openings. In contrast, the inner façades are highly transparent.

Ten cottages, each housing eight women, are arranged around the green and linked to the central complex with pedestrian pathways and a circular drive. The cottages are expressed in a simple language of residential and agrarian references — deep porches, sloped roofs and rustic materials — to respond to the rural setting.

Throughout the complex, the design fosters positive relationships, encouraging choice and self-sufficiency in small but meaningful ways — from individual kitchens, to operable windows for natural ventilation, and free-standing, loose furniture that can be reorganized to reflect individual preference and changing activities.

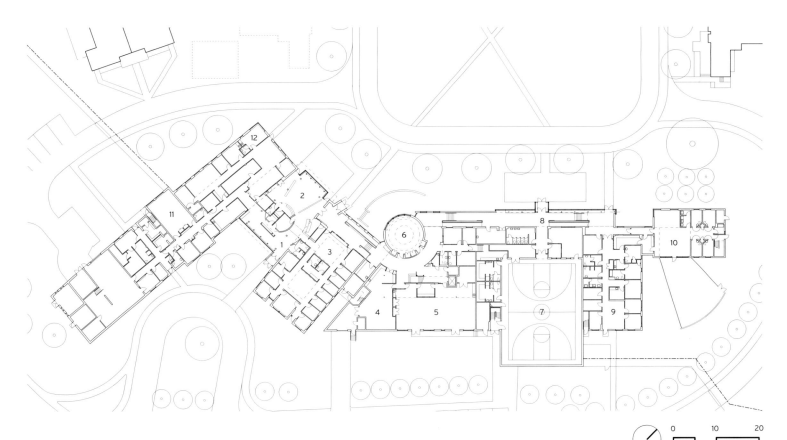

ABOVE: Interiors of the main building are detailed to minimize the institutional nature of the project, and to emphasize exposure to natural light. The spaces are stepped down to respond to the topography of the site and include the loggia/corridor lined with benches (LEFT), and a visitation room (CENTRE). The stair across the lobby from the spirituality room is detailed in a modern idiom (RIGHT).

OPPOSITE: Each house accommodates eight women residents who are responsible for daily chores from laundry to ordering supplies and cooking meals. Front porches reinforce the residential character of the complex.

Main building, ground floor

1 entrance
2 visiting
3 case management
4 food distribution
5 vocational training
6 spirituality room
7 gymnasium
8 loggia/corridor
9 health care
10 special security
11 administration
12 warden

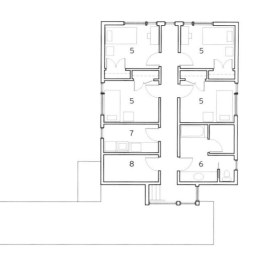

Residential unit, ground floor

Second floor

1   porch
2   kitchen
3   dining
4   living
5   bedroom
6   washroom
7   laundry
8   storage

Ammirati Puris Lintas

1997 NEW YORK

The New York advertising agency Ammirati Puris established its reputation with the launch of "The Ultimate Driving Machine" campaign for
BMW in 1974. Twenty years later, in 1994, the agency merged with
Lintas Worldwide to form Ammirati Puris Lintas (APL). The New York
staff of both agencies was relocated to 1 Dag Hammarskjöld Plaza
located opposite the United Nations Building. The project involved the
transformation of ten dark, labyrinthine floors of office space into a
light-filled, open office environment and established a prototype for
APL offices worldwide.

The plan conceptually extends the urban geography of avenues,
streets and squares. Entrance/reception sequences and primary
circulation routes terminate as framed views of the United Nations
Headquarters, the East River and the New York skyline. Perforated steel
partition screens demarcate interconnecting stairs, which are cut
into the floor plate to facilitate vertical circulation and communication
between floors. Within this plan order, a series of flexible modules
for executive offices, standard offices and open workstations facilitate
the organizational reconfigurability of integrated work spaces.

The resultant template combines the economic use of white drywall,
industrial grade grey carpet and prefabricated elements with the selec-
tive deployment of natural materials such as beechwood, perforated
metal and Carrara marble for custom-made reception desks, credenzas,
screens and cabinets. The overall effect creates a loft-like gallery environment to function as a backdrop to the agency's range of creative,
research and account functions.

Typical floor plan

1 elevator lobby
2 reception
3 conference room
4 office
5 workstation
6 video conference room
7 client waiting area

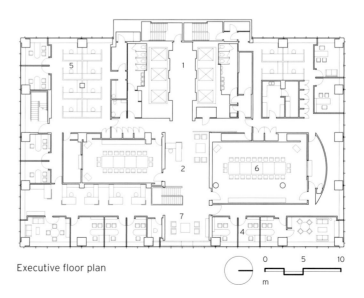

Executive floor plan

ABOVE: Client waiting area.

OPPOSITE: Detail of steel-supported staircase
with partition screen.

Japanese Canadian Cultural Centre

2000 TORONTO

This project involved the adaptive re-use of an existing office building and printing plant into a vibrant community centre to support a program of traditional and contemporary Japanese activities. The design creates a flexible infrastructure that combines new construction and strategic renovation over a phased series of interventions.

Three elements — sign, screen and lantern tower — create a recognizable presence for the centre on its new site. A large steel and cedarwood screen wraps the south-east corner of the building and visually directs the arrival sequence. The main entrance is marked by a translucent glass and steel tower which formally recalls the Akari lamps designed by Isamu Noguchi.

A long east-west Gallery Street reorganizes the interior plan order and creates a multi-functional space in which cultural, historical and social programs converge. The Gallery Street is designed for maximum flexibility to accommodate receptions and special events, a permanent exhibition gallery and general spaces for casual meeting.

To draw natural light into the deep horizontal plate of the ground floor plan, large floor-to-ceiling windows were inserted at the end of the Gallery Street, which also frame views to the exterior courtyard garden. Wood and glass screens along the Street are inspired by traditional shoji screens.

Front elevation facing south

0   5   10   15

m

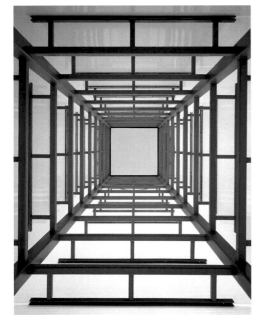

Hilton Toronto
2000 TORONTO

This project involved the transformation of an existing hotel built in 1975 into a flagship for Hilton Hotels (Canada) and represents the international hotel chain's initiative to shed its formerly conservative image in response to the changing needs of the hospitality industry and the rising expectations of business and leisure travelers.

The program called for the renovation of twenty-seven floors of guest rooms and public areas, including the lobby, mezzanines and third floor meeting rooms overlooking the atrium. The architectural solution began by peeling back the existing fabric of the public areas to reveal the simplicity and elegance of the original concrete structure. In the lobby, existing pre-cast concrete cladding was stripped down to its bare surface and sandblasted to a smooth, polished texture.

The lobby plays a central role in the overall concept. Metaphorically, it was envisioned as a stage set, with an elevated lounge. Diaphanous scrims and wood and metal screens perform much like set pieces, defining precincts of movement and repose. A series of back-lit, fabric-wrapped 25-foot columns line the atrium's spine, amplifying the spatial grandeur of the lobby. A suspended staircase of glass, onyx and steel improves vertical circulation between the mezzanine and ground floor lobby. Cantilevered over the existing escalator, the stair is positioned as a figural element within the overall order. A translucent blue glass bridge connects two sections of the original mezzanine, and is intermittently animated by the silhouettes of guests moving across the atrium.

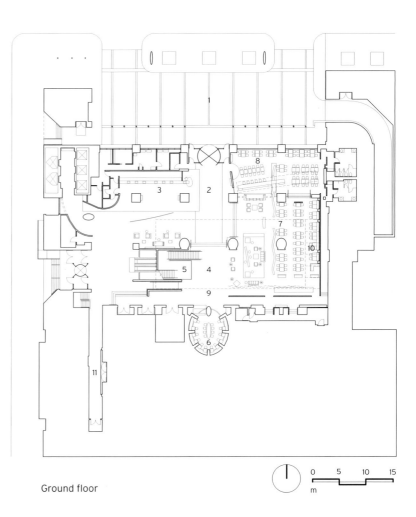

1   arrival court
2   main entrance
3   front desk
4   lobby
5   stair to mezzanine
6   coffee bar
7   restaurant
8   bar
9   mezzanine above
10 glass bridge above
11 retail corridor — existing

Ground floor

0   5   10   15
m

ABOVE: View of lobby.

RIGHT: View from reception desk, with screen element of engineered walnut planks and canted, powder-coated steel pipes.

85

ABOVE: View of lobby from front entrance and
cantilevered stair with backlit onyx balustrade.

RIGHT: Glass bridge and mezzanine with walnut
and marble credenza.

Cardinal Ambrozic Houses of Providence

2000 SCARBOROUGH, ONTARIO

The Cardinal Ambrozic Houses of Providence are a 288-bed addition to the existing Providence Centre, a health-care facility offering outreach, ambulatory and residential services for the frail elderly and chronically ill. This residential project represents a new prototype in long-term care which transcends the institutional environment typical of these facilities with an environment that prioritizes community exchange, individual choice and responsive care.

To the north end of the existing facility, the new building is configured as two four-storey L-shaped wings that flank a central pavilion to form a new north entrance court. Each wing defines a secure courtyard landscape with therapeutic gardens and continuously looped paths that safely accommodate wandering Alzheimer patients. The expression of the building deliberately borrows from a domestic vernacular with references to bay windows, chimneys, porches and pitched roofs. The central pavilion contains the heart of the building, the Great Hall, a double-height space for social and recreational activities and special amenities including a chapel, café, beauty/barber shop and a general store. The typical floor is conceived as a "house." Each house accommodates eighteen individual resident rooms, with a communal living/dining zone and a spa area.

The individual room represents the key element in the mandate to deinstitutionalize the long-term care environment. A large, low, deep window focuses the plan of each room and functions as a source of natural light, view and connection to the world. In this sense, the window is the symbolic nucleus of the project and recalls how the proportions and position of the windows in Alvar Aalto's Tuberculosis Sanatorium in Paimio (1933) permit a person lying in bed unobstructed views to the outside. A memory box, with a customized display case and shelf, marks each entrance, encourages personalization and provides a recognition device for the elderly.

This project was completed as a joint venture of Montgomery and Sisam Architects and Kuwabara Payne McKenna Blumberg Architects for Providence Centre.

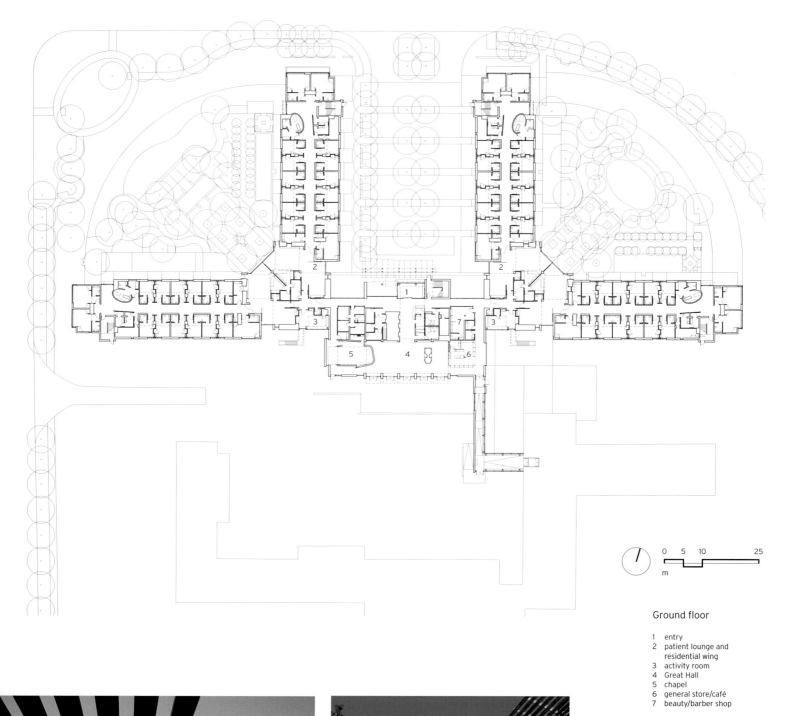

Ground floor

1 entry
2 patient lounge and
  residential wing
3 activity room
4 Great Hall
5 chapel
6 general store/café
7 beauty/barber shop

OPPOSITE: Courtyards and therapeutic gardens.

ABOVE: Great Hall (LEFT). Resident's room (RIGHT, TOP). Memory box (RIGHT, BOTTOM).

Richmond City Hall

2000 RICHMOND, BRITISH COLUMBIA

Located south of Vancouver on the delta of the Fraser River, Richmond was originally founded as a farming and fishing community. It is now one of British Columbia's fastest developing municipalities. As part of the city's long-term vision to situate Richmond as a viable urban centre, the architecture of the City Hall transforms a generally unexceptional suburban site bounded by high-speed traffic corridors into an accessible and identifiable civic precinct.

Built on the original site of the 1919 Town Hall, and replacing the former 1957 building, the new city hall extends Richmond's tradition of civic meeting space. The project is characterized as an ensemble of three buildings which enclose a Civic Square and configure a network of landscaped outdoor courtyards. By breaking down the overall massing into three precincts, functional activities are clarified and flexibility in operations and environmental efficiency is maximized.

At the forefront of the grouping, the circular Council Chamber is located at the south-east edge of the site in proximity to the street, its glazed perimeter encouraging observation and civic participation. Immediately to its north is an eight-storey administrative tower, its exterior a composition of horizontal bands of clear and spandrel glass offset by two fully-glazed outbound fire-exit stair towers. Conceived as generously scaled, naturally lit spaces, the towers were designed to reduce elevator use and to encourage vertical circulation and inter-departmental communication.

The horizontal, two-storey Meeting House anchors the Council Chamber and the tower on the east end and extends west as the primary circulation spine through the site. Its two-storey, glass and timber framed galleria projects to the exterior, defining primary entrances at the east and west ends. As the main organizing element, the Meeting House links together interior program components as well as outdoor courtyards and gardens.

Each floor has access to exterior balconies and terraces. South-facing exterior horizontal louvres control solar gain. Porcelain-fritted glass is used on the west façade to minimize excessive heat gain. Natural ventilation is achieved through operable windows and a hybrid ventilation system allows workers to control their environmental comfort levels.

The landscape concept integrates existing heritage trees and low-maintenance plant materials. The topography of cascading water features and extensive berming creates an abstract network of landforms and vegetation, evoking symbolic references to Richmond's indigenous terrain.

This project was an association of Hotson Bakker Architects and Kuwabara Payne McKenna Blumberg Architects.

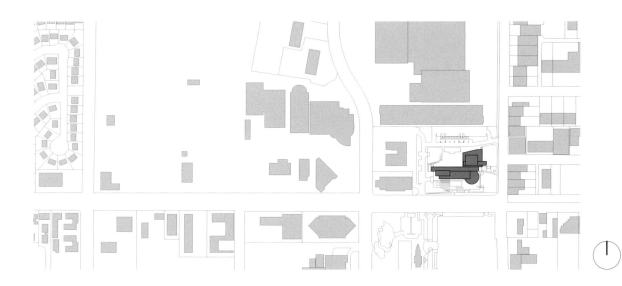

94

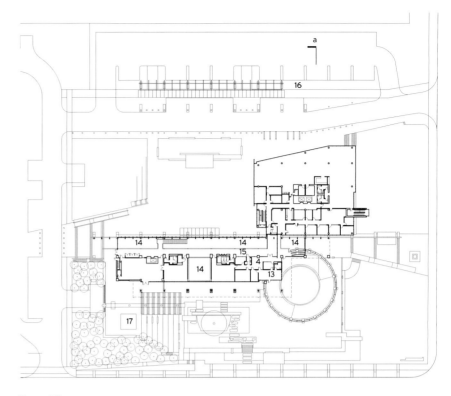

Second floor

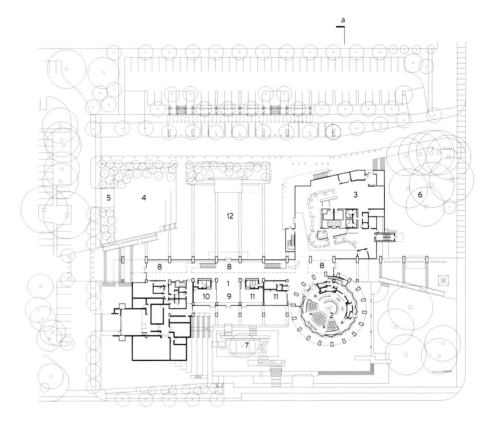

1   Meeting House
2   Council Chamber
3   administrative block
4   west lawn
5   entrance to below grade parking
6   east lawn
7   south terrace and water gardens
8   galleria
9   atrium
10 café
11 meeting hall
12 terrace
13 mayor's office
14 open to below
15 galleria walkway
16 north canopy
17 west terraces and tree grove
18 Brighouse Park

Ground floor

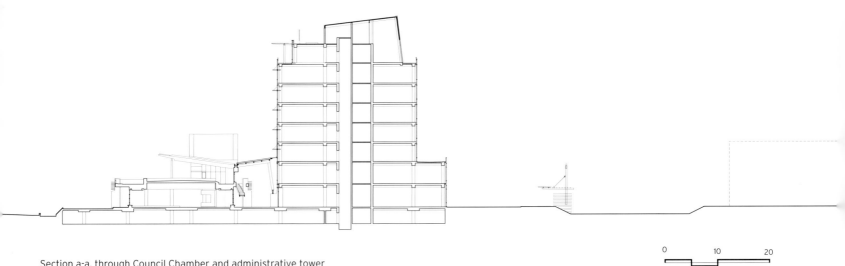

Section a-a, through Council Chamber and administrative tower

0   10   20
m

ABOVE: Meeting House with glass and timber galleria.
RIGHT: Council Chamber with glazed perimeter.

OPPOSITE: The structural order of the Meeting Hall reflects a clear material sequence. The roof is supported by a Douglas fir frame and connected to a continuous steel beam which rests on a base of solid concrete piers.

Goodman Theater

2000 CHICAGO

Distinguished by a number of Tony Award winning plays, the Goodman
Theater is one of Chicago's renowned repertory theatres. The new
Goodman Theater is located on a half block that is bounded on the
north by Lake Street, the south by West Randolphe Street and on the
east by Dearborn Street. The project fronts City Hall Plaza and is next
to the EL line. The site comprises an empty lot and the abandoned
Selwyn and Harris theater building.

The architecture responds to the adjacent heritage theatre buildings.
The scale of the new theatre is deliberately contrasted to the scale
of surrounding high-rise towers to distinguish the Goodman Theater as
an artistic institution within its new urban context. The design establishes contiguity with the history and character of Chicago's original
theatre district and promotes the future development of the area as
a revitalized cultural precinct.

A solid masonry plane is suspended above the façade of the new
theatre on Dearborn. Dramatic lighting, entrance canopies and banners
create an atmosphere of spectacle and drama, transforming the urban
streetscape into a space of performance.

The project was completed by Kuwabara Payne McKenna Blumberg Architects in
association with DLK Architecture Inc. and McClier Corporation.

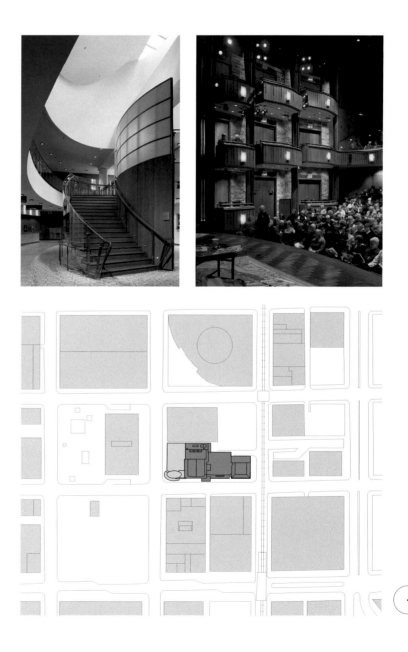

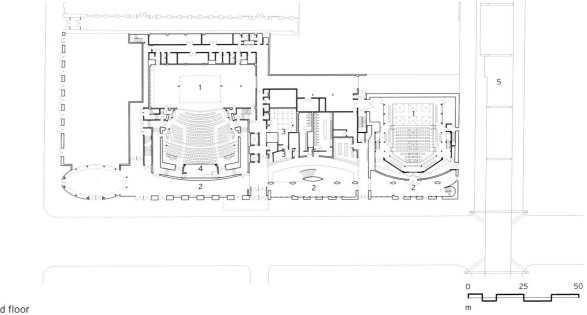

1 stage area
2 lobby
3 ticket booth
4 control room
5 The EL

Ground floor

0   25   50
m

Ravine House

2001 TORONTO

Occupying the edge of one of Toronto's oldest forest ravine systems, this house reinterprets the principles of traditional modernism associated with domestic architecture of the early twentieth century within the building constraints of the Canadian climate. Built on the splayed footprint of a pre-existing 1950s bungalow to minimize impact on the natural terrain and to maintain as-of-right approvals with respect to proximity to the ravine, the house deliberately occupies a small percentage of the site. A back-lit fence anchors the house to the landscape and conforms to the ordinance of the city's grid. Constructed of horizontal teakwood slats and an interior zinc liner, the fence acts as a singular, unifying element that encloses the length of the property and defines a spatial field against which the house and outdoor spaces are composed.

The house is conceived as a pair of two-storey masonry volumes intersected by a single-storey pavilion building clad in mahogany wood siding, and pivoted to form an L-shaped courtyard dwelling with diagonal views to the ravine. The vertical volumes contain the private, hermetic spaces of the house while the pavilion contains an interconnected space where dining/living and kitchen/service functions flow together to support daily activities and family and social gatherings. The front exterior is opaque and deliberately understated. In contrast, the façade of the forecourt emphasizes translucency and openness to encourage the infusion of architecture with nature. The courtyard, with its outdoor fireplace and wood decks, is a mirrored extension of the interconnected levels of the interior living and dining spaces.

The authenticity and functionality of materials as load-bearing devices is emphasized in the overall scheme. A hybrid structural system combines conventional wood framing with localized steel framing for cantilevered projections and entrance canopies. Doors and windows are custom profiles milled from mahogany finished with a dark stain. The soffits of large overhangs are white exterior grade plaster with galvanized aluminum edge and roof flashings. Ontario limestone is used for exterior walkways and courtyard surfaces. The interior material palette is limited to hardwood elm floors, plaster skim-coat drywall and stainless steel flatbar. Millwork elements, composed of an enclosing frame of mahogany with articulated units finished in wengewood, perform as spatial modifiers. Black firebrick is used for fireplaces; honed and flamed Ontario limestone is used for hearths and mantels.

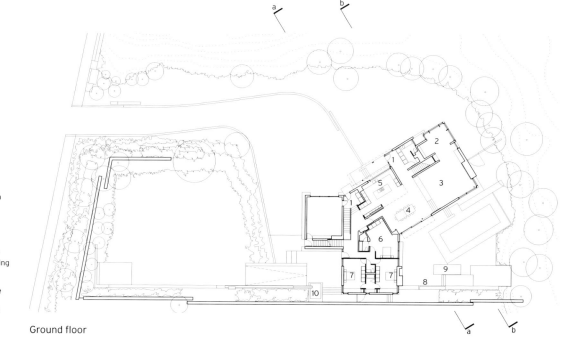

1   entry
2   library and
    sitting room
3   living room
4   dining
5   kitchen
6   guest room
7   bedroom
8   outdoor bar
9   outdoor dining
10 fountain
11 den
12 master suite
13 dressing
14 family room

Ground floor

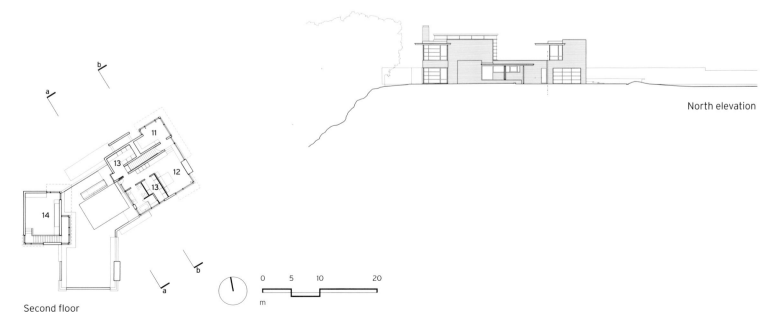

North elevation

Second floor

Section a-a

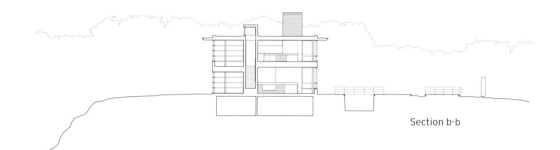

Section b-b

ABOVE AND LEFT: The open plan of the central pavilion is unified under a continuous ceiling plane. Dining, living and kitchen zones are defined by custom millwork elements and sliding screens.

RIGHT: Stair leading to master suite and den, with a stainless steel flatbar handrail.

Jackson-Triggs Niagara Estate Winery

2001 NIAGARA-ON-THE-LAKE, ONTARIO

The winery district of the Niagara Peninsula in Southern Ontario is an unusually fertile region characterized by the Niagara Escarpment, a geographical formation that causes mild air to circulate across the land, making possible the cultivation of vineyards in this northern climate. Over the last decades, the region has significantly improved the quality of its wine and has become an important tourist destination. Typically, the wineries in the district have evolved from production facilities and have stylistically mimicked European precedents of the château and bodega. The Jackson-Triggs Estate winery created an opportunity to merge contemporary wine-making technologies with an authentic architectural response to the region.

The design reflects on agricultural typologies characteristic of Southern Ontario as well as the French notion of *terroir*, which suggests that the features of a terrain impart unique qualities to the wine. The extended horizontal form is sited parallel to the Escarpment and unites production and hospitality functions under a continuous roof supported by full-span wood trusses. The building footprint is minimized by locating barrel cellars, storage and warehouse facilities in the basement level below the fermentation cellar and public spaces, thus maximizing space for vineyard production and facilitating gravity flow for the wine-making process, a significant factor in the making of premium wine.

The linear scheme maximizes exposure to north and south light. The substantial overhang of the roof eliminates excessive solar gain, and operable windows create naturally ventilated spaces, eliminating the need for mechanical cooling requirements through summer months. Mechanical systems are reduced to one cooling plant that provides both air-conditioning and process cooling to respond to seasonal temperatures.

In keeping with the notion of *terroir*, materials (stone, wood, and steel) are left in their natural state, with finishes restricted to clear sealers. The building is framed in structural steel and clad in oversized cement board (clapboard). Exterior walls reinterpret the local vernacular of fieldstone bases with the substitution of low-cost, discarded strata from the regional quarry beds of the northern tip of the Escarpment.

The gravity flow system was adapted as a metaphor for the choreography of the winery tour to allow visitors to follow the process of 'grapes to wine' while allowing production to be kept separate from public access. The plan is divided into the two main sections of the working winery and hospitality facilities and connected by a double-storey, convertible Great Hall. From the Great Hall, visitors ascend an exterior ramp to the two-storey fermentation cellar where a series of suspended catwalks provide viewing platforms to the stacked stainless steel fermentation tanks. From the fermentation cellar, visitors descend to the barrel cellar, and re-ascend to conclude the tour in the tasting gallery.

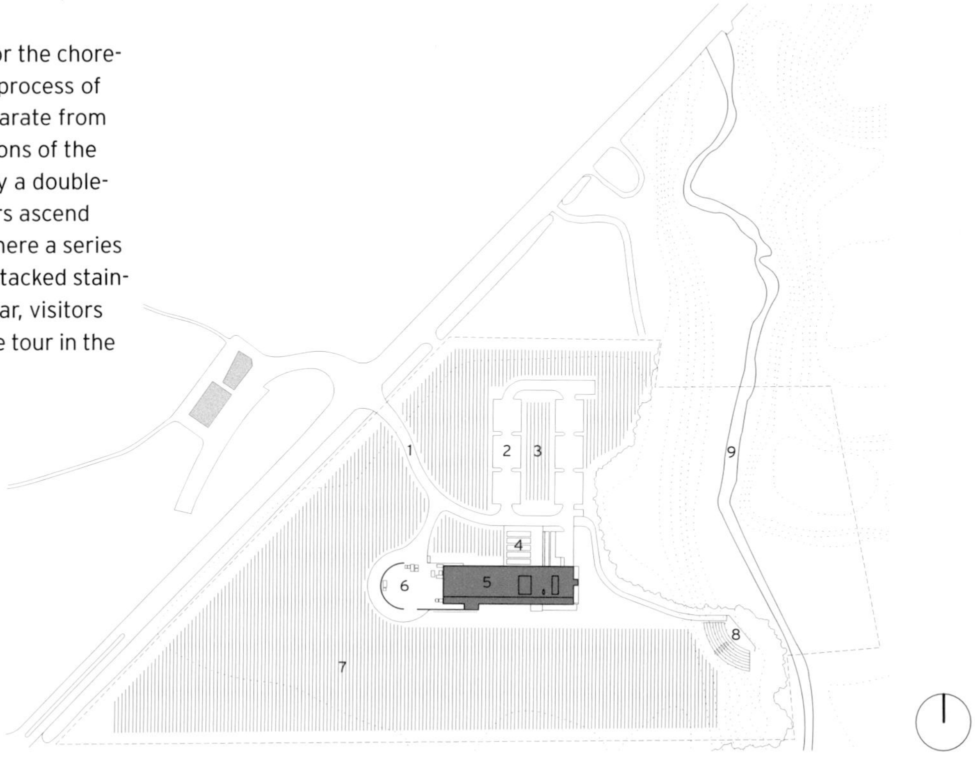

1 entrance drive
2 parking
3 demonstration vineyard
4 gardens
5 winery
6 service court
7 vineyard
8 outdoor amphitheatre
9 Two Mile Creek

RIGHT: A two-level water trough runs along the eastern edge of the entry court and leads into the convertible space of the double-height Great Hall equipped with 20-foot-high motorized glass doors.

OPPOSITE: Various views of the Great Hall stair and fireplace.

A long ramp leads to the fermentation cellar (OPPOSITE, ABOVE) which features 60-foot clear-span, inverted Douglas fir trusses. The trusses extend through the clerestorey glazing to support the roof overhang and also eliminate the need for columns, achieving maximum stacking space for the fermentation tanks.

1 great hall
2 pedestrian ramp
3 viewing platform
4 pressing mezzanine
5 production catwalks
6 bridge
7 office/administration
8 boardroom/dining
9 terrace
10 VIP lounge and tasting
11 service court
12 crushing and pressing area
13 fermentation area
14 storage (loading dock)
15 retail shop
16 tasting gallery
17 wine bar and tasting room
18 wine maker's office/laboratory
19 staff lounge
20 fountain

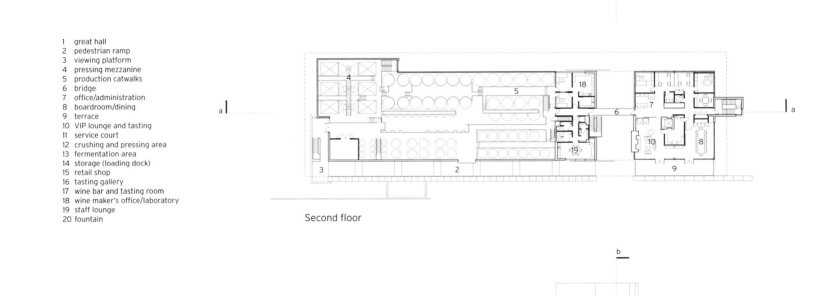

Second floor

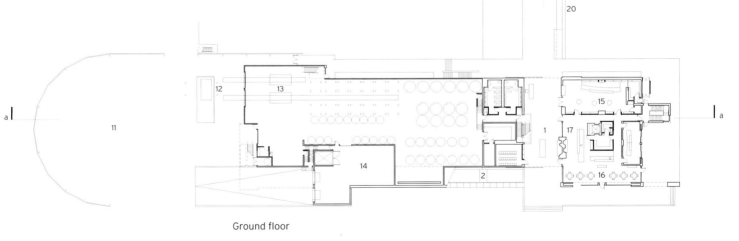

Ground floor

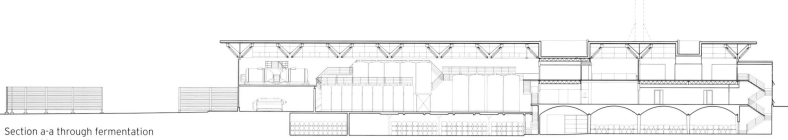

Section a-a through fermentation
area and barrel cellar

ABOVE: The barrel cellar is distinguished by a vaulted
ceiling. The heat sink effect of the surrounding
earth maintains the stable, cool and humid environment ideal for barrel aging.

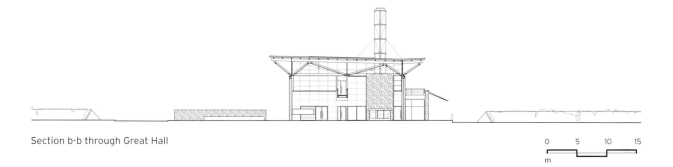

Section b-b through Great Hall

0 5 10 15
m

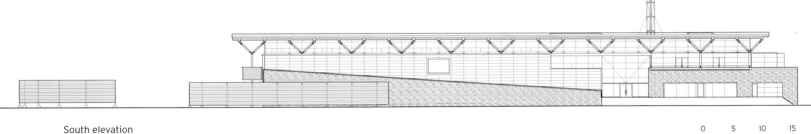

South elevation

0 5 10 15
m

ABOVE: The boardroom and VIP lounge, located on
the upper level, use indigenous white oak for floors
and custom millwork.

RIGHT: Aerial view of winery with
Lake Ontario in the distance.

Star Alliance Lounge

2001 ZURICH INTERNATIONAL AIRPORT, SWITZERLAND

This project was the winning scheme in an anonymous international design competition to develop a prototypical lounge concept for Star Alliance™, the largest global network of airline carriers. The objective was to establish a strong brand identity that would attract frequent fliers, while being easily adapted to airports around the world. The 7,700-square foot prototype, located in Zurich International Airport, accommodates 130 patrons in business class and 30 in first class.

The design concept creates an urban garden — a calm, warm and sensual space consisting of a series of micro-environments in which passengers can relax or work between flights. Two interchangeable signature elements define the lounge — a central pavilion and a slatted wood screen. The interior is finished in stone and wood, the selection of which is responsive to regional preferences and availability.

The slatted maple screen, or "garden wall," defines the entrance and allows controlled degrees of transparency from the lounge reception area into the business class section. The reception desk, with its back-drop of a floor-to-ceiling image of the earth, is positioned to greet visitors directly. The garden wall incorporates food service bars and a television viewing area, and functions as both a psychological enclosure for the interior and as a unifying element that anchors the plan.

The central pavilion is a raised platform beneath a suspended birchwood ceiling and is framed by screens of slatted walnut and woven stainless steel mesh. The pavilion maximizes viewing opportunities to the perimeter windows. A promenade around the pavilion forms a continuous zone of movement, services and seating, while the screens define more secluded, intimate zones.

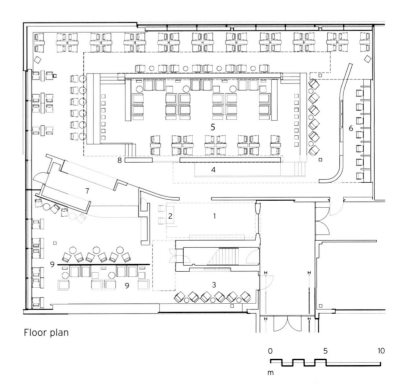

1 lobby
2 reception
3 first class lounge
4 ramp
5 gold lounge
6 work stations
7 servery
8 mesh screen
9 walnut screen

Floor plan

0   5   10

m

OPPOSITE, TOP: A separate section for workstations is visually and acoustically separated from the rest of the lounge by the garden wall.

ABOVE: A continuous zone of seating, services and circulation encompasses the central pavilion. The floor is finished in flame-cut slabs of piasentina stone.

Roy Thomson Hall Enhancement
2002 TORONTO

Home to the internationally acclaimed Toronto Symphony Orchestra,
Roy Thomson Hall first opened its doors to the public in 1982. Designed
by Arthur Erickson, it was hailed as a new architectural and cultural
icon. One of the unique features of the concert hall was the large volume of space in the auditorium, but this proved to be acoustically prob-
lematic for the performers and patrons. The inherent shortcomings
in the natural acoustics of the auditorium prompted the development
of an enhancement program that would transform the venue into a
world-calibre concert hall and multi-purpose facility while respecting
the integrity of Erickson's architectural concept.

The hall's acoustical problems were remedied by altering the shape
and decreasing the volume of the hall. This was accomplished by bringing in the side walls of the upper chambers with a series of wooden
bulkheads to reconfigure the original oval shape of the auditorium into
a smaller, more rectilinear sound chamber and by lowering the ceiling
with a pair of adjustable acoustical canopies to allow volume and
sound distribution to be optimized according to the scale of each
performance. Other interventions included the addition of retractable
sound-absorbent banners for use during amplified performances,
a more resonant stage floor and surround walls at the stage, which
enhance the acoustic environment for performers.

The bulkheads, located along the sides and back of the hall above
the upper balcony seating, were designed as curved wood panels to
follow the original form of the concrete walls, and stepped down incre-
mentally to follow the existing balconies. The bulkheads bring the
walls approximately fifteen feet in and reduce the interior volume by
13.5%, making it comparable to the interior volume of Carnegie Hall in
New York. The exposed surfaces of the wooden panels are five-inch-
thick timber panels with a maple veneer. The panels were fabricated in
sections and suspended from three-tiered steel frames that are hung
from the roof trusses and braced to the concrete walls. The tops of
the bulkheads were installed eighty feet in the air, utilizing a crane that
was disassembled and reassembled in the centre of the hall.

The height of the hall is reduced by two ceiling canopies: a main
circular canopy approximately fifty-five feet in diameter and a crescent-
shaped canopy with a sixty-four-foot diameter. In addition to reducing
the volume of the hall, the canopies act as sound deflectors, and
depending on the type of performance the height can be raised to ten
feet from the ceiling or lowered to seven feet from the stage. The
canopies contain catwalks used to access various lighting systems as
well as a handrail system that doubles as support for state-of-the-art
performance lighting. Although fabricated in segments and bolted
together on site, the canopies are continuous steel frameworks designed
with structural redundancy. The steel framework is enhanced with
maple cladding and onyx light fixtures.

The consistent use of Canadian white maple for the new interventions introduces a layer of warmth and sensuality to complement yet
stand apart from Erickson's original palette of concrete, soft greys,
and chrome.

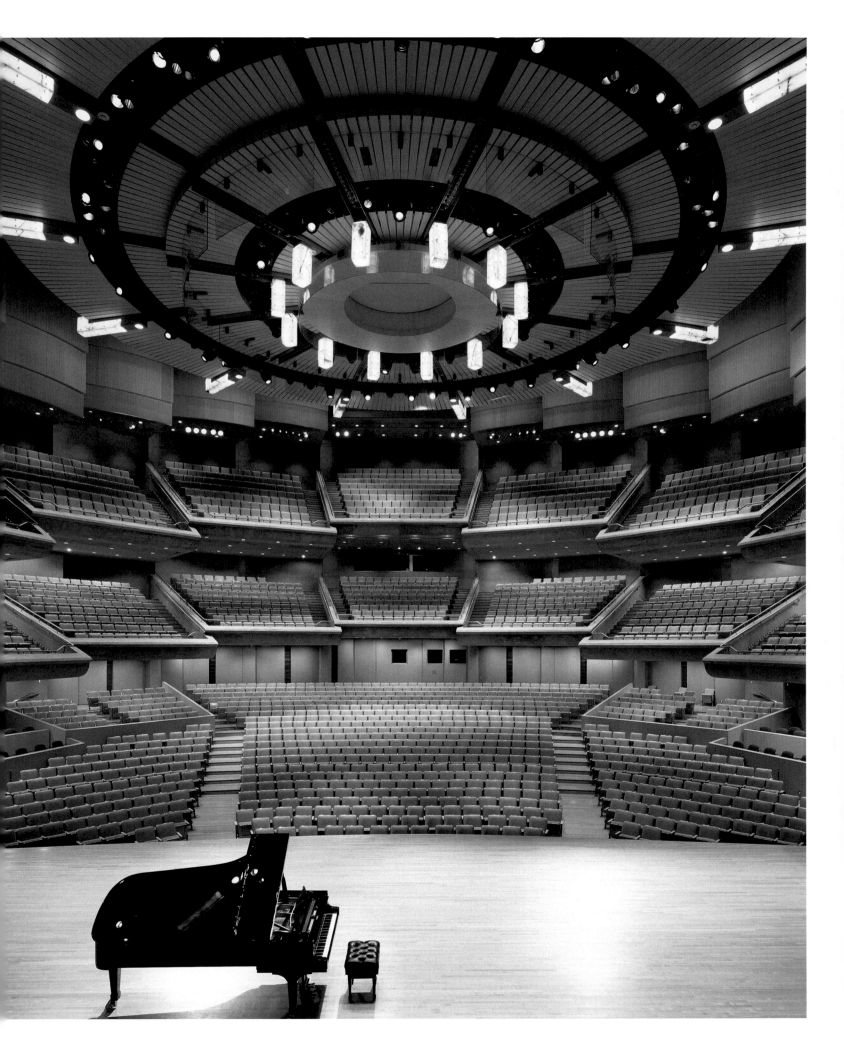

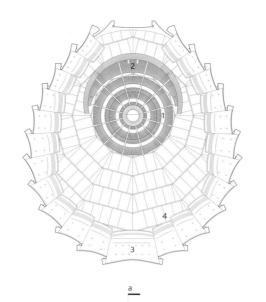

Reflected ceiling plan canopy

1 main canopy
2 crescent canopy
3 new bulkheads faced with wood planking
4 retractable banners

a

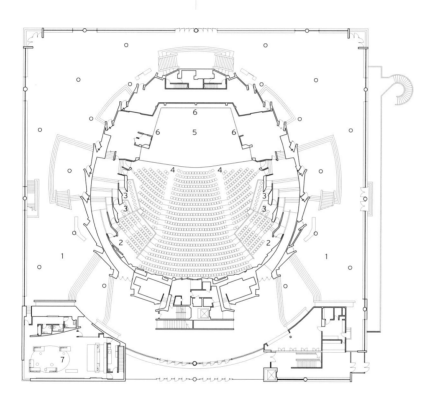

Orchestra level plan

1 lobby
2 parterre
3 box seats
4 new aisle
5 stage
6 pivot acoustic panels
7 Maestro's lounge

a

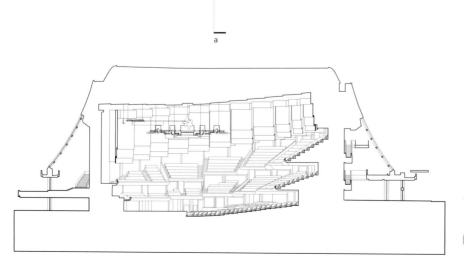

Section a-a, through hall with
canopy at high trim

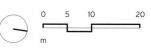

0   5   10   20

m

Lexus Lounge, Roy Thomson Hall
2004 TORONTO

Following the enhancements to the Roy Thomson
Hall auditorium, a former double-height rehearsal
hall was transformed into new revenue-generating
space. A concrete floor slab was inserted at the
upper lobby level, creating two functional rooms.
The upper level was adapted as a private lounge
for patrons and donors, and the lower level creates
a multi-purpose meeting space.

   The space was the sole opaque section of the
otherwise fully glazed perimeter. In order to visually
connect the lounge to the street, the corner was
opened up with new full-height glazing inserted into
the concrete wall. The interior walls are clad with
large square panels of the same sandblasted maple
used for the auditorium enhancement. The curved
forms of the original building are echoed in the arc
of the ebony-clad feature wall and the sculptural
form of the bar. Furnishings are deliberately minimal
to maximize standing room during intermissions.

Genomics and Proteomics Research Building, McGill University

2003 MONTRÉAL

This project consolidates Canada's knowledge and research base in the fields of genetic and proteomic technologies and gene therapies under one roof. The new building also houses the Montréal Bone Centre and incorporates five distinct bio-incubators to encourage start-up companies in related fields of research. Inspired by the collaborative nature of the Human Genome Project, where genetic researchers from around the world share their findings on a daily basis over the Internet, the architectural resolution, a metaphor for the scientific process, is conceptualized as an incubator for research, emphasizing visual accessibility and innovation.

Located on Avenue Dr. Penfield, in the science and technology precinct of McGill University's downtown campus, this six-storey building is simultaneously an urban infill project and a singular form. Sited between the historic Strathcona Anatomy Building and the Wong Engineering Building to the south, its western façade is aligned with the neighbouring buildings. The building's scale is modified by articulating its overall mass as a three-storey metal-framed glass "research box" perched on a masonry base, and capped with a metal-clad penthouse. The two-storey 'contextual' limestone base is built of reclaimed stone from the Donner Research Building that formerly occupied the site. The lower two floors, expressed as a piano nobile, are pushed forward to create a large, elevated terrace on the campus side. The "research box" houses the three levels of the Genomics Centre and Proteomics Research Laboratories which are accessed by a glass-enclosed interconnecting staircase.

The plan is organized by a central north-south corridor and bisected with a multi-storey atrium. The lower atrium extends from the principal entrance at Penfield and descends to the campus level on the east, creating an indoor public route between the city and campus. The enclosed staircase at Penfield connects to the upper three-storey atrium, around which are organized lounges and the teleconference room. Laboratories are located on the east. The spaces where the collected data is processed and analyzed are located on the west. Offices and meeting rooms are canted to create a series of angled rooms with views to Mont Royal. The teleconference room is expressed as an oculus on the west elevation, and acts as a symbol of the global nature and significance of genetic research, enabling a virtual connection to the international research community.

As the conceptual surface for bio-scientific exploration, the material and optic qualities of glass — as reflector, irradiator and projector of light and motion — are explored throughout the scheme.

This project is a joint venture of Kuwabara Payne McKenna Blumberg Architects and Fichten Soiferman et Associés, Architectes, Montréal.

ABOVE AND RIGHT: Fenestration patterns create abstract surfaces that play on the theme of genetics, and refer to the elemental building blocks of DNA. On the west façade, a layer of canted planes clad with mesh scrim filter the glare of the low-altitude afternoon sun and conceal a random pattern of window openings which are revealed at dusk.

OPPOSITE: On the east façade, the mullion pattern maps out a formal plan transparency to reveal the building's genetic code: the locations of interior walls and laboratory spaces are projected to the exterior where walls are delineated by mullions of various sizes and configurations, and coded to signify enclosed office spaces with dark blue glass, and open spaces with green glass.

138

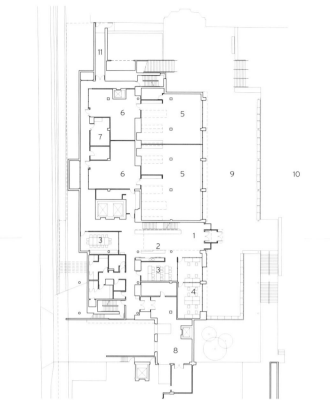

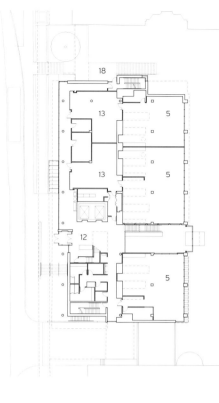

Level 3   Level 4   Level 6

```
        0    5    10         20
        _____
    m
```

1 lower atrium/campus entrance
2 café
3 conference room
4 training centre
5 bioincubator laboratories
6 bioincubator offices
7 sterilization (shared)
8 loading dock/storage
9 exterior terrace
10 Tomlinson Square
11 Link to Strathcona Building
12 lower atrium/Penfield entrance
13 bioinformatic offices
14 upper atrium/stair
15 teleconference room
16 private offices (bioinformatics)
17 open office (bioinformatics)
18 academic offices (shared)
19 laboratory
20 robotics room
21 x-ray laboratory
22 equipment room

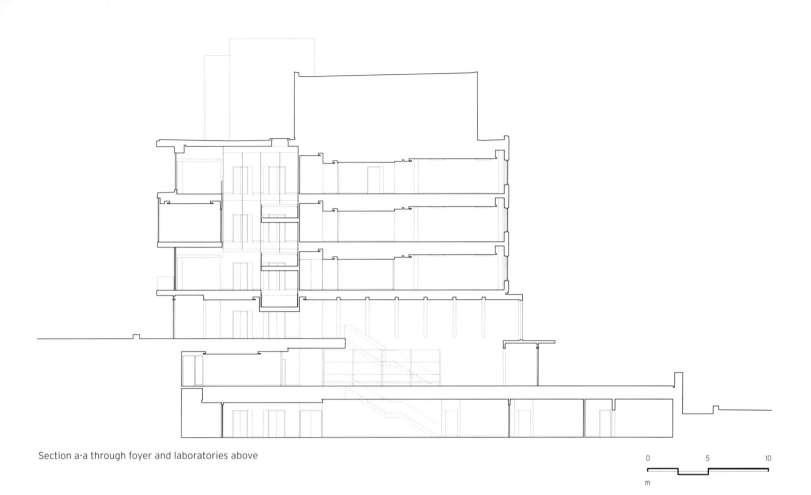

Section a-a through foyer and laboratories above

0 5 10
m

ABOVE: The public route through the building leads past an onyx reception desk and the sculptural form of an enclosed stair at the west entrance, and continues down a stair to the east entrance on the campus side (RIGHT).

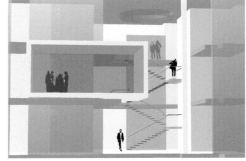

ABOVE AND OPPOSITE: The volumes of the enclosed stair and the teleconference room intersect the three-storey atrium.

Raether Library and Information Technology Center, Trinity College

2003 HARTFORD, CONNECTICUT

Trinity College is a small liberal arts college distinguished by an ambitious masterplan prepared by the English architect William Burges in 1873–74 with his American colleague Francis H. Kimball. It was intended as one of New England's largest university buildings, aspiring to the scale of Oxford and Cambridge, and represents an early example of North American Collegiate Gothic architecture. The proposal called for three interconnected quadrangles enclosed by buildings. However, the only part of the plan that was built was a 700-foot-long structure, known today as The Long Walk, which was eventually expanded into a U-shaped form with the addition of new buildings over the course of the nineteenth and twentieth centuries.

The library project builds on the recommendations of a new masterplan prepared in 1997 by Cooper, Robertson Ltd. to elevate the college's academic standing in contemporary scholarship and enhance its architectural status within the urban fabric of Hartford. It involved the seamless integration of a new construction with two existing, stylistically incongruent buildings: a red brick and sandstone structure with pitched slate roofs (1952) and a four-storey, flat roof building clad in dark gray granite (1977).

The new construction, situated at the end of the nineteenth-century Collegiate Gothic complex, is an extension of the heritage structure and defines a new arrival courtyard with a two-storey cloistered arcade connecting it to the neighbouring Austin Arts Center. Resonant with the heritage campus buildings, a common material palette of local red brick, vineyard red sandstone and brownstone is used to unify existing and new structures.

The new five-storey addition is linked to the existing buildings by a three-storey glass-enclosed atrium and a principal north-south circulation spine which defines the main entrance. The dense masonry wall of the 1952 structure was opened up to connect visually and spatially through the building. The program's reading, study and research spaces are organized around the atrium and accessed vertically by a cantilevered staircase which sits beneath a blue rimmed ocular skylight. A double-height reading room reinterprets the tradition of great reading rooms, while reading alcoves along the perimeter create more intimately scaled study spaces.

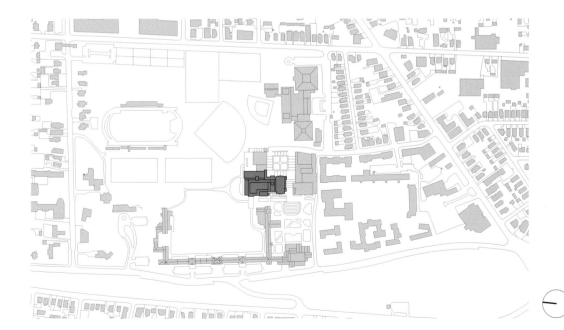

RIGHT: Main entrances are illuminated with custom light fixtures crafted in bronze, stainless steel and acrylic.

145

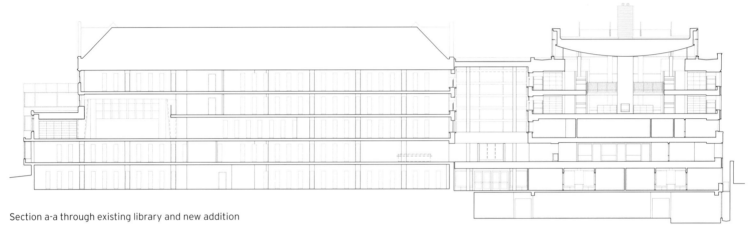

Section a-a through existing library and new addition

Section b-b through new addition

0   5   10
m

ABOVE: A cloister wraps the new and pre-existing portions of the facility. The exterior material palette consists of split-faced and cut red sandstone, brownstone and red brick to match the existing buildings, painted steel, and aluminum and wood details.

OPPOSITE: The double-height reading room is lined at the perimeter with intimately scaled reading rooms clad in white oak. The ceiling and fireplace are finished in Venetian plaster.

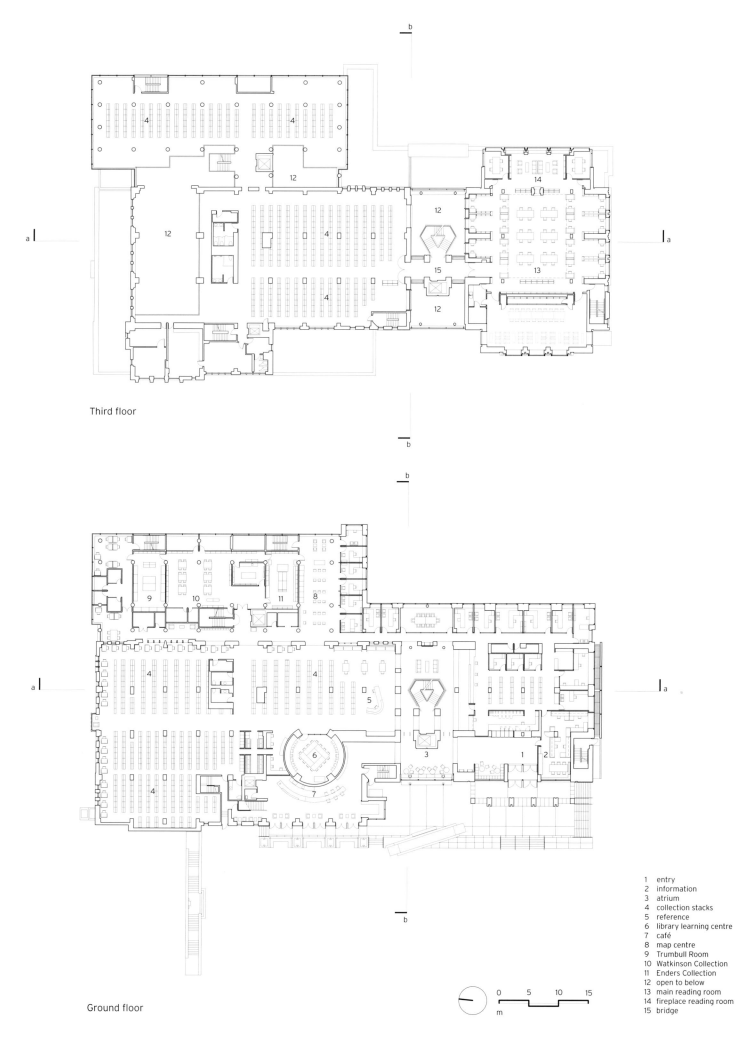

Third floor

Ground floor

1   entry
2   information
3   atrium
4   collection stacks
5   reference
6   library learning centre
7   café
8   map centre
9   Trumbull Room
10   Watkinson Collection
11   Enders Collection
12   open to below
13   main reading room
14   fireplace reading room
15   bridge

0   5   10   15
m

ABOVE AND RIGHT: A four-storey atrium bridges the renovated and new areas of the library and features a cantilevered triangular staircase with a solid oak balustrade. The staircase is positioned beneath an ocular skylight with a deep blue Venetian plaster rim.

James Stewart Centre for Mathematics, McMaster University

2003 HAMILTON, ONTARIO

The James Stewart Centre for Mathematics involved the adaptive re-use of Hamilton Hall (1929), one of the oldest buildings on the McMaster University campus. Originally designed to house the sciences department, the building was spatially alienated from its original function and reconfigured into a student centre in the 1960s. James Stewart, a mathematician and committed alumnus of the university, donated funds to transform the interior of Hamilton Hall into a centre for mathematical excellence, thereby reverting the building — since mathematics is known as the 'original science' — to its original purpose.

The concept deliberately imposes a highly abstract modern interior in stark opposition to the traditional exterior. The solution involved the dissolution of the dark, labyrinthine interior with the insertion of a new skin behind the existing stone façade. The complete interior demolition resulted in exposing the concrete post-and-beam construction beneath the Collegiate Gothic façade of the original building. By removing sections of the floor slabs, an architectural void was inserted to unify the space vertically and horizontally. The constructed void, articulated in blue glass, visually connects the building's four storeys. Skylit openings at its east and west limits allow natural light to be drawn deep into the interior spaces. As a visual incision, the void is occupied by light and space and functions as a tangible surface and volume, the objective correlative of the reception and distribution of ideas.

Individual faculty offices and graduate study areas are located along the building's perimeter. The existing stone-framed Gothic windows are the nuclei around which each office is organized. The offices are unified under a continuous ceiling plate that allows the existing concrete beams and slab to define the full spatial extents. Horizontal glass slots on office fronts draw light into hallways from the perimeter openings.

In contrast to the hermetic quality of the offices, public corridors are oversized and furnished with tables and benches to encourage group study and collaborative thinking. Slate blackboards, devoted to recording mathematical notations yet susceptible to less scientific graffiti, are woven through the office and corridor spaces.

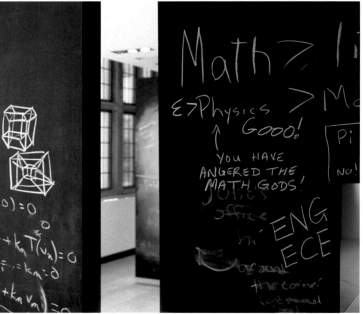

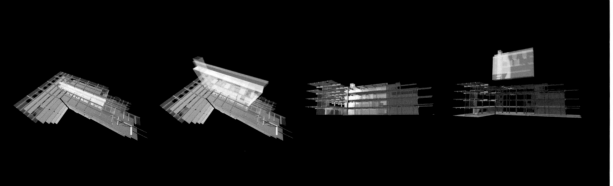

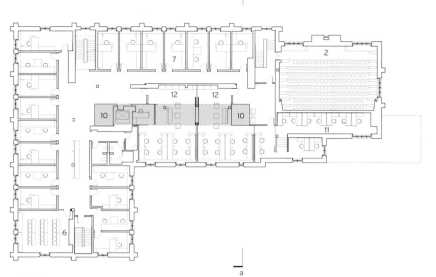

Third floor

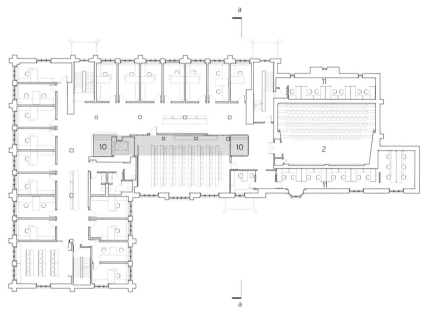

Second floor

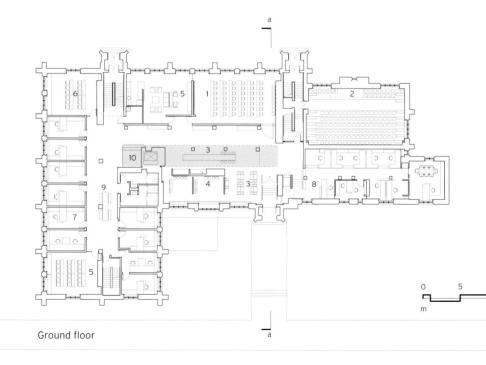

Ground floor

1 colloquium room
2 lecture hall
3 café
4 tutorial area
5 department lounge
6 seminar room
7 faculty offices
8 administration
9 tutorial
10 open to below
11 graduate student offices
12 math labs

0   5   10
m

The project provides two types of space conducive
to the practice of mathematics: individual offices
for focused thinking (OPPOSITE, TOP), and generous
corridors and lounges where ideas are shared (ABOVE
AND OPPOSITE, BOTTOM).

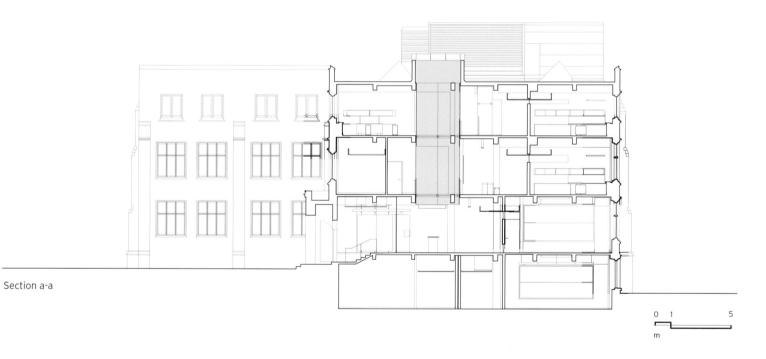

Section a-a

0 1   5
m

OPPOSITE: The constructed blue glass void provides
a spatial and visual connection between the four
levels of the building.

St. Andrew's College

2003 AURORA, ONTARIO

This private boarding school for boys was established in Toronto in 1899. In 1925, it was relocated north to the village of Aurora, now a growing town to the north and east of downtown Toronto. Located on a 110-acre forested site within the rolling farmland of the Oak Ridges Moraine, the College is distinguished by its pastoral landscape and the heritage character of its red brick Georgian Revival buildings.

The St. Andrew's College tradition is based on a well-rounded approach to the critical development of the mind, body, heart and spirit of every student. Entering into the twenty-first century, the College recognized that the physical environment needed to keep pace with the constant enrichment of the academic offering in order to reinforce and strengthen St. Andrew's leading edge reputation, while responding effectively and inventively to the phasing out of the Ontario Grade 13 program.

The new masterplan developed by KPMB evolved from the original 1926 Marani and Morris campus plan, and re-establishes the orthogonal grid of the Georgian Revival campus, which had been shifted off axis with a series of modern brick buildings built in the 1960s and 70s. An under-utilized exterior space between the heritage Dunlap Hall and the Dunlap Gymnasium was enclosed with a timber roof and clerestorey to create an indoor court and a new heart for the campus. The original Dunlap Gymnasium was converted into an art studio facility and creates an improved learning environment that reinforces the lively and well-established art program as a core subject of St. Andrew's curriculum.

In response to the increased enrolment of day students, the new site plan concept reroutes vehicles away from the historic buildings and creates an improved drop-off zone and new entrance. Two new buildings — the Middle School for Grade 6 and 7 students and their gymnasium — define this new North Court, as well as the Amphitheatre Courtyard to the south. To harmonize with the character of the heritage structures, the buildings are articulated in red brick and Manitoba Tyndall stone, with copper detailing. The overall massing of the new gymnasium structure is reduced by carefully setting it into the natural campus landscape and preserving existing coniferous tree groupings. Wiarton stone paving, ipewood screens and stainless steel railings underline the permanence and quality of the existing campus while expressing the spirit of the new.

The architecture of the Middle School emphasizes natural light, reinforces transparency and creates well-lit, acoustically balanced classrooms that optimize visual and physical connections to the natural landscape.

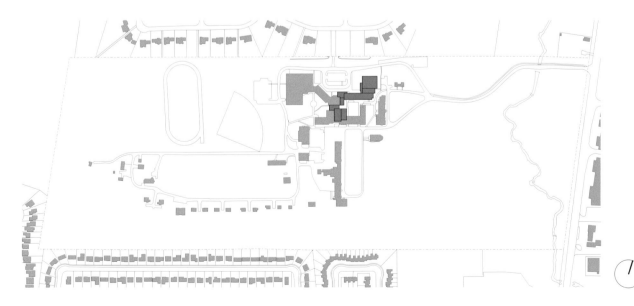

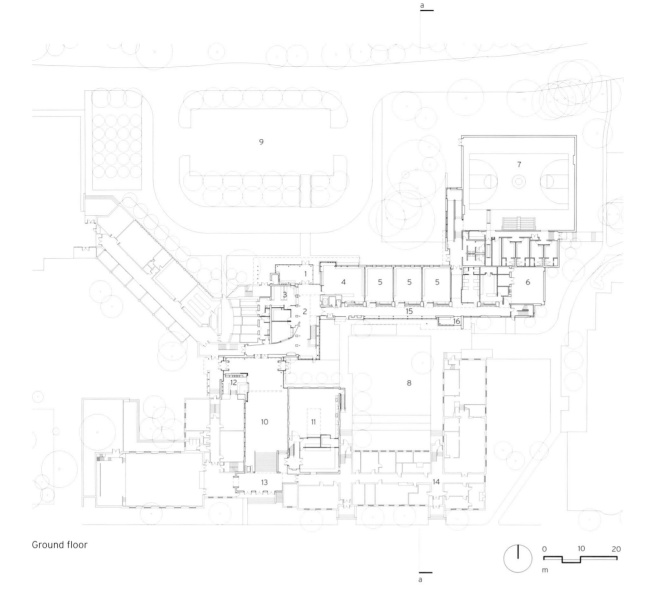

Ground floor

1 entry hall of new middle school
2 corridor
3 administration
4 resource room
5 classroom
6 multi-purpose room
7 gymnasium
8 outdoor amphitheatre
9 parking court
10 great hall/court
11 art facility
12 retail
13 original entrance
14 Dunlap Hall

OPPOSITE: In each classroom, windows are located both on exterior and interior walls. Smaller openings in side walls create a visual enfilade of views through the length of the building.

ABOVE: Hallways are lined with continuous oak benches.

RIGHT: Ramp leading to middle school gymnasium.

North elevation

South elevation

Section a-a through new Middle School and Outdoor Amphitheatre

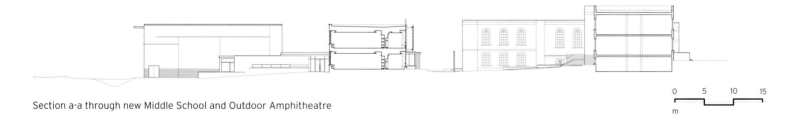

0   5   10   15
m

ABOVE: The gymnasium was converted into an art studio.

OPPOSITE: An under-utilized exterior space between Dunlap Hall and the original gymnasium was enclosed with a timber roof and clerestorey to create an indoor court and new heart for the campus.

Sprague Memorial Hall, Yale University

2003 NEW HAVEN, CONNECTICUT

Sprague Memorial Hall, a 1917 neoclassical building, occupies the geographic center of the Yale School of Music. The mandate was to preserve the treasured acoustics of the original building while improving amenities and environmental conditions to meet the standards of quality offered by the university's programs.

The improvements to the 650-seat recital hall include a control booth and technical upgrades to make the hall adaptable to a greater diversity of musical genres, including opera. The project also involved the creation of new office space, practice studios, classrooms, and two acoustically specialized suites for recording and electronic music. To improve the thermal comfort of the building, while respecting the original character, contemporary HVAC and performance lighting systems and a state-of-the-art public address system were carefully integrated into the existing structure. An existing freight elevator was replaced with a larger elevator to facilitate the movement of instruments, particularly pianos, from the stage to practice rooms in the lower levels of the building. New windows, modeled on the original windows, were installed to isolate exterior noise. A modern performance production lighting system was installed as a continuous sidewall lighting bar that merges with the Hall's cornice.

The plan was clarified to improve the arrival sequence, including the reconfiguration of the lobby with a new box office and the introduction of a new oval-shaped Green Room. Changes to the exterior were limited to the introduction of pole-mounted luminaries and the re-creation of historic playbill cabinets affixed to the building for an improved communication infrastructure.

Aesthetic enhancements included the restoration of plaster relief patterns and decorative bronze fixtures. The introduction of gilding for ornamental detail draws out the latent drama of the building, generating visual delight. Refinements, such as the refinished blond wood stage floor and the new dark blue upholstered seats, are harmonized with the existing architectural character.

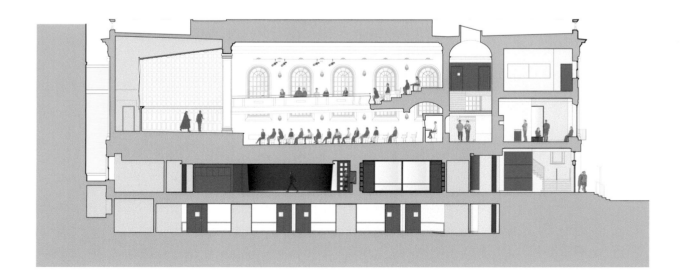

RIGHT: The exterior of the egress stairway added between Sprague Hall and the adjacent Harkness Building is clad in lead-coated copper and features a 20-foot-high window with teakwood frames and a combination of clear and cast amber *glass lites*.

Centennial HP Science and Technology Centre, Centennial College

2004 SCARBOROUGH, ONTARIO

Founded in 1966, Centennial College implemented the Province of Ontario's community college system as an alternative to university education offering career-oriented training to students leaving high school. The new Hewlett Packard (HP) Science and Technology Centre represents the first phase in the development of a formal and mature campus for Centennial that replaces the typical high school model with an innovative, sustainable academic village concept. Located on lands owned by the University of Toronto and leased to Centennial, this project is part of a larger government initiative to generate greater synchronicity between college and university systems in Ontario. The design focuses three priorities: to create a revitalized image for Centennial, to promote the public realm as an active learning environment and to demonstrate ecological leadership in the local community.

Located on the north-east corner of Ellesmere and Morningside Avenues, the building is composed as two extended horizontal wings, each oriented parallel to its respective thoroughfare. The Morningside wing opens to views of the Highland Creek forest area and the city to the south. The main entrance court occurs at the point where the two wings meet, and leads into the heart of the building — an indoor "town square." A suspended volume, clad in Douglas fir and containing a lecture hall, is the focus of the town square. A wide stair mirrors the angled underbelly of the volume. Conceived in the spirit of the Spanish Steps, the amphitheatre-like stair leads to a lounge/café below and creates a flexible indoor space for casual as well as formal assemblies.

Centennial's programs respond directly to industry demands. In order to accommodate ongoing innovations to the curriculum and anticipate changing technologies, the plan is organized as a flexible loft, based on a twenty-by-forty-foot structural grid of bays running the full length of each wing, with academic space organized along each side of a wide central sky-lit atria zone. The raised floor system allows for the easy reconfiguration of spaces to respond to changing technologies and programs while the atria create a coherent public infrastructure of light-filled circulation spaces that culminate in a series of zones occupied by lounges, cafés and open teaching areas with optimal views of the surrounding landscape. The network of atria also supports the college's requirement for sustainability by allowing for the incorporation of operable windows on the perimeter and achieving natural ventilation through the stack effect.

The material palette is raw, industrial and economically-driven, maximizing the use of exposed concrete. Exterior façades are variegated, ranging from prefabricated black corrugated steel siding on the north and east, to dark charcoal brick and aluminum on the west. Apart from wood cladding on the exterior of the lecture hall volume, the interior is primarily exposed concrete and painted drywall.

The HP Science and Technology Centre is an association of Kuwabara Payne McKenna Blumberg Architects and Stone McQuire Vogt Architects.

Ground floor

Second floor

1 entrance
2 student commons
3 amphitheatre/seating terraces
4 cafeteria
5 resource centre
6 classrooms
7 exterior courtyard
8 reception
9 atria
10 labs
11 lecture theatre
12 offices
13 lounge

0 10 20 30
m

Third floor

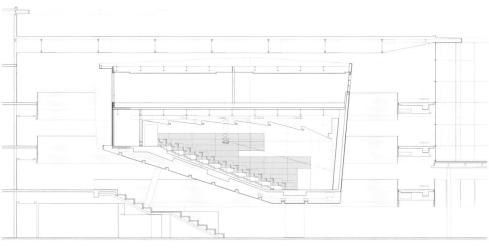

Section through lecture theatre

ABOVE AND OPPOSITE:
North and east elevations.

Centennial HP Science and Technology Centre, Centennial College

Work in Progress

Canadian Embassy

FALL 2004 BERLIN, GERMANY

The winning submission in a national design competition, the new Canadian Embassy in Berlin occupies an important site at the junction of Leipziger Platz and Potsdamer Platz. The Embassy occupies the first four floors of the Leipziger Platz block and all floors of the Ebert-strasse block, as well as the penthouse which provides views to the Reichstag, Tiergarten and Brandenburg Gate. The commercial component is situated on Vossstrasse, while the residential component occupies the upper floors of the Leipziger Platz block overlooking the Platz. The design of the Embassy conforms to the stringent planning and design guidelines set out by the District Office of Central Berlin.

The building acts as a bridge between the park setting of Leipziger Platz and the active mixed-use transportation interchange of Potsdamer Platz. A public route, the Canada Passage, proceeds through the site between Leipziger Platz and Ebertstrasse. The building's openness and accessibility is an expression of Canada's commitment to democracy. The plan configuration forms an interior courtyard, which is occupied by the centrally located, sky-lit decahedral Timber Hall.

On axis with the Leipziger Platz entrance, the ground level of Timber Hall will function as an exhibition room and accommodate a variety of events from public gatherings to exclusive diplomatic functions. A conference facility, located on the second level, is accessed by a grand circular stairway.

The material palette of wood and stone is derived from several regions of Canada, while other materials are selected for their German content: for example, zinc from Germany is used for the exterior cladding, while the interior is lined with Douglas fir from British Columbia and floors are clear maple from Quebec. The building's material expression creates a subtle interplay between the diversity and plurality of the Canadian identity and the specificity of its presence in Berlin. The landscape concept was developed with Cornelia Oberlander and includes a green/glass roof.

The Canadian Embassy is a joint venture of Kuwabara Payne McKenna Blumberg Architects; Gagnon Letellier Cyr, Architectes; and Smith Carter Architects and Engineers Inc.

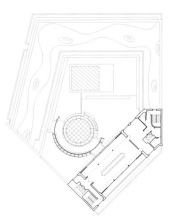

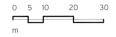

Roof

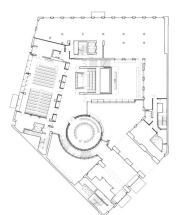

Second floor

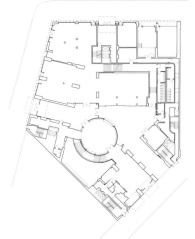

Ground floor

OPPOSITE, TOP: View of Timber Hall under construction.

OPPOSITE, BOTTOM: Renderings of the Leipziger Platz façade and courtyard with Canada Passage and exterior of Timber Hall.

Le Quartier Concordia, Concordia University

2005 MONTRÉAL

The downtown campus of Concordia University is conceived as a comprehensive but loosely organized assemblage of buildings that occupy a significant zone of Montréal's urban core. The project was the winning scheme in a design competition that required the creation of an integrated urban campus that would play a significant role in revitalizing and repositioning the University's rank and reputation.

Occupying a limited footprint of a full city block, the design creates a vertical campus of three faculty buildings — the Molson School of Business and the faculties of Engineering/Computer Science and Visual Arts. The composition is loosely configured as a family of individual yet related architectural forms. Figurative canopies project off the roofs of each building and create a distinctive urban campus skyline. The roof canopies of the Engineering/Computer Science building and the John Molson School of Business define symbolic gateways along Guy Street to the campus.

The Visual Arts Building, located along Ste-Catherine Street, is defined by an active street frontage consisting of a café, an outdoor sculpture court, galleries and an art supply store, which extend the retail strip of Ste-Catherine further west. Its robust form and lower profile create a flexible loft building that relates to the industrial structures of the city. In contrast, the School of Business is streamlined and more corporate in character. It is conceived as a secretariat-type building housing a combination of teaching and working space.

The interior concourses create active ground planes which extend to the street, and are interconnected with the existing Guy-Metro (CB) building and the underground metro system. Lower levels will contain an experimental black box theatre, laboratories and an athletic complex, as well as a new home for Hexagram, a centre for excellence in digital media.

Small, stacked atria with spiral stairs organize interior vertical circulation routes. The stairs are an iconic reference to the vernacular of Montréal's townhouses. Shared lounges and glass-fronted meeting spaces are positioned adjacent to the atria to maximize interchange between students and faculty.

This project is a joint venture of Kuwabara Payne McKenna Blumberg Architects and Fichten Soiferman et Associés, Architectes.

Ground floor

0 10 20 30 50
m

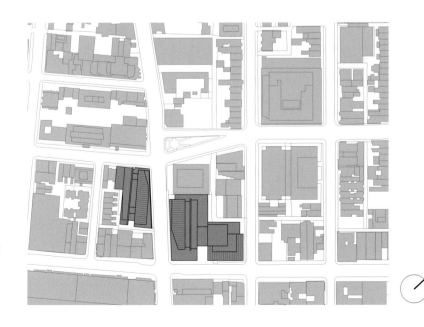

Gardiner Museum of Ceramic Art

2005 TORONTO

The Gardiner Museum is one of the world's pre-eminent institutions devoted to ceramic art, and the only museum of its kind in Canada. Located opposite the Royal Ontario Museum and around the corner from the Royal Conservatory of Music, the Gardiner occupies a significant presence in one of Toronto's growing cultural precincts. The expansion and renovations will ensure its continued success as a relevant and contributing public institution.

Within the existing building, the program accommodates a new entrance vestibule, an expanded museum shop and a contemporary ceramics gallery. The existing gallery space is reorganized to accommodate a circuit of galleries and a multi-purpose lecture hall. Below-grade parking is transformed into four flexible ceramic studios.

Additional space is provided with a third floor built above the existing concrete frame structure of 1984, which was originally designed to anticipate vertical expansion. This addition is expressed as a light-filled pavilion and accommodates temporary exhibition space, a restaurant and event space, and also provides access to roof terraces. The need for a public elevator and larger entry court resulted in removing an existing stairway which dominated the interior view from the entrance, and provided the opportunity to create a more generous, ceremonial entrance experience. Two new volumes with glass façades extend the original footprint and are situated between the existing Gardiner and the neoclassical façade of the Lillian Massey building to the north. These volumes link into the basement level.

The reconfiguration of the front elevation with the new framed and glazed second floor projection extends the original façade to the street, creating a more distinctive urban presence for the museum. A new light grey limestone skin seamlessly wraps existing and expanded spaces together, and transitions into a screen of limestone solar louvres over the glazed spaces of the upper floors. The overall composition of new additions and exterior courts and terraces is conceptualized against the niche of neoclassical and Queen Anne style buildings that encompass the museum to its north and east.

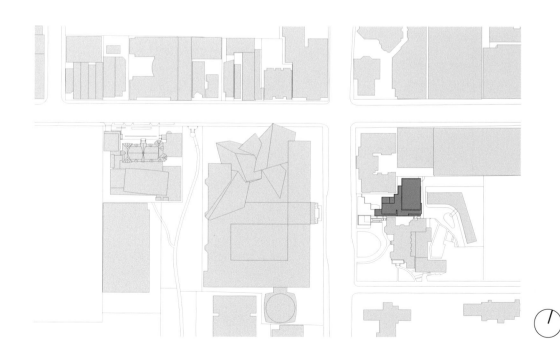

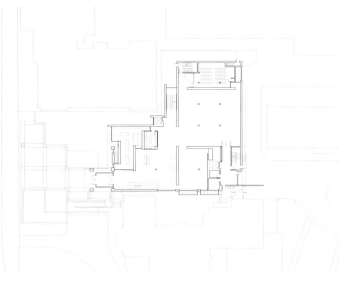

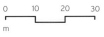

Ground floor

Third floor

Royal Conservatory of Music
Performance and Learning Centre
2006 TORONTO

The Royal Conservatory of Music (RCM), founded in 1886, is Canada's premier music and arts educator. Since the 1960s, the RCM has been housed in two Victorian buildings: McMaster Hall (1881) and Mazzoleni Hall (1910), which was restored and converted into a concert hall by KPMB in 1997. Located on Bloor Street West, Toronto's main east-west artery and high-end shopping district, the RCM occupies an important urban site adjacent to the Royal Ontario Museum (ROM). In concert with Daniel Libeskind's transformation of the ROM, and KPMB's work on the Gardiner Museum of Ceramic Art, the expansion and restoration of the RCM will define a new cultural centre for Toronto.

The RCM is surrounded on three sides by University of Toronto properties, including Philosopher's Walk, a landscaped route which runs north-south from Bloor Street along the RCM site. The new additions are assembled around McMaster Hall, and scaled to respect the heritage context. The concept is structured around the idea of creating great rooms for music performance and brings together three concert spaces — the existing Mazzoleni Hall, a new Rehearsal Room and the new Concert Hall — within the framework of the Performance and Learning Centre. The centre piece is the 1,000-seat concert hall that will match international standards for world calibre acoustics.

An entrance court is formed by the addition of a North Pavilion fronting Bloor Street, to the west of McMaster Hall. The footprint of the new Concert Hall is parallel and to the south of McMaster Hall. A sky-lit court connects the heritage and new structures, and creates a central circulation and gathering space. A three-storey lobby positioned to the east of McMaster Hall and two levels of bridges connect the west wing back to the heritage structure.

The Concert Hall is a large classical "shoe box" form, with an undulating wood acoustic overlay. An acoustic canopy above the stage curves upward to form a floating ceiling element. Wood ribbons below the canopy extend beyond its edge and create a floating intermediate ceiling.

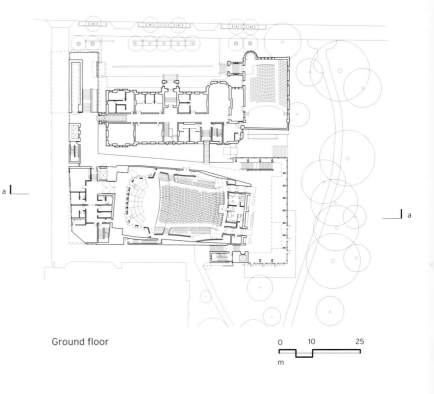

Ground floor

0   10   25
m

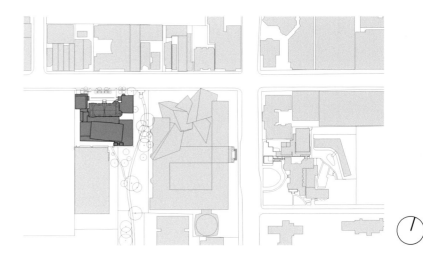

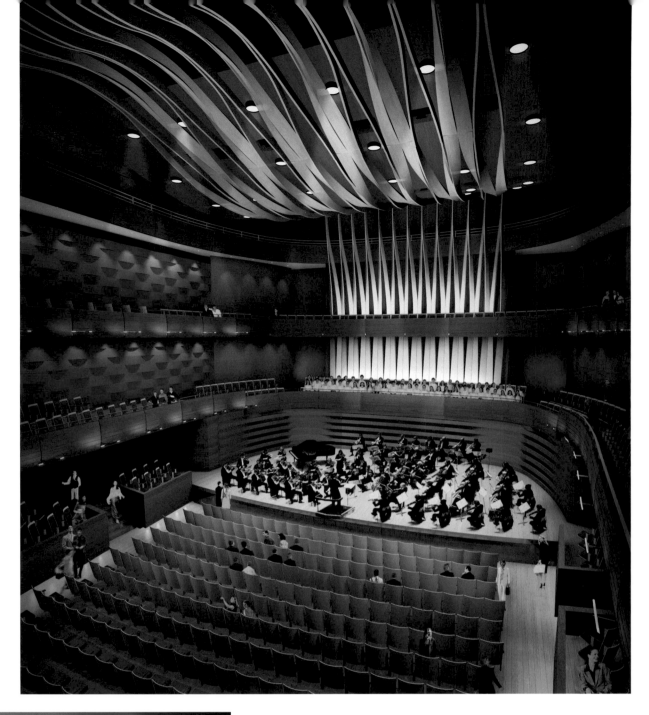

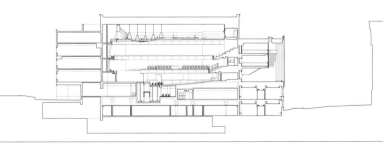

Section a-a through concert hall

Young Centre for the Performing Arts
2005 TORONTO

This multi-purpose theatre and training facility is the result of a joint venture of the Soulpepper Theatre Company and George Brown College. The venture between the two organizations marries the growing renown of Soulpepper and their commitment to educating young performers with George Brown College's reputable theatre programs. The project will realize a home, shared rehearsal and support facilities and unique venues for live theatre which both organizations currently lack.

The project will occupy the historic Gooderham & Worts Distillery complex, specifically the Tank Houses 9 and 10, and the exterior court-yard spaces created between them. The existing buildings are both single-storey brick warehouse structures with existing floors at grade level. The interventionist scheme will include a 400-seat flexible theatre, a 200-seat flexible format dance theatre, three 100-seat studio theatres, rehearsal/teaching studios, performance support spaces, workshop facilities, lobby and ticketing facilities, and administrative offices for both organizations. The design envisions the renovation of the two Tank House buildings and the creation of a link building between them with lobby spaces and a 100-seat studio theatre.

The overall concept evolved within a strict budget and was driven by the historic context and respect for the patina of the existing buildings. The majority of new construction will consist of reclaimed materials. With the exception of a new canopy over the main entrance, new interventions are limited to large glazed surfaces and massive Douglas fir timber beams for roof trusses. Finishes for interior public and theatre spaces are utilitarian. Floors are concrete, and existing walls are left exposed.

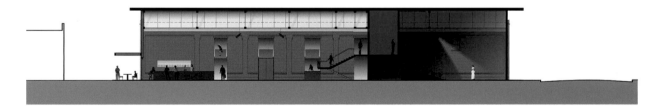

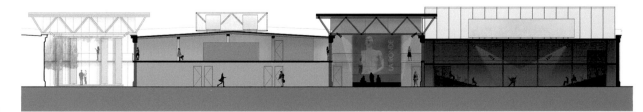

Early sectional studies

Festival Centre and Tower
Toronto International Film Festival Group
2008 TORONTO

The Toronto International Film Festival resonates with the city's growing status as an international centre for the film industry. The Festival
is widely recognized as the most important annual film festival after
Cannes and the most successful public film festival in the world. The
cultural and economic impact of the Festival is immense, creating a
substantial and vital influx of tourism and business every September.
The new Festival Centre and related condominium tower are conceived
as a reflection of the heterogeneity and optimism of Toronto's evolving urban image. The design concept creates a hybrid building that
combines a permanent home for the Toronto International Film Festival Group (TIFFG) within a five-storey street-related base building and
an adjacent 42-storey residential point tower. It will occupy an undevel-
oped lot at the intersection of the John Street media corridor and the
King Street theatre district.

The Festival building is configured as a series of platforms that
express the diversity of TIFFG's program mix. The façade of the building is activated by an assemblage of volumes and planes. A super-sized,
luminous marquee projects over the King Street entrance. An arcade
extends from the John and King Street intersection to the main entrance. Its canopy is punctuated with a series of lens-like skylights that
borrow exterior light sources from the street. A carpet of moving images
guides visitors to the entrance, from which a path lined with floor lights
will lead into the lobby and box office. Inside, a central atrium defines
an urban stage for film screenings and galas. The roof is articulated as
an outdoor amphitheatre for screenings and formally references the
roof of the Villa Malaparte, an icon of film and architecture.

The form and expression of the condominium tower borrows from
the language and proportions of modernist office towers of the 1950s
and 60s to create a clean, simple and contemporary figure on the city's
skyline. From a distance, the Festival Tower will become an extension of
Toronto's silhouette of skyscrapers that are clustered within the financial core to the east. The building envelope and balconies are fully
glazed. The design of the exterior treatment will explore the material
and optic qualities of glass to articulate a random pattern of degrees
of transparency.

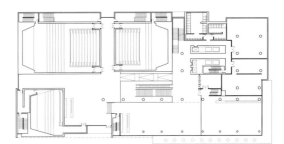

Second floor

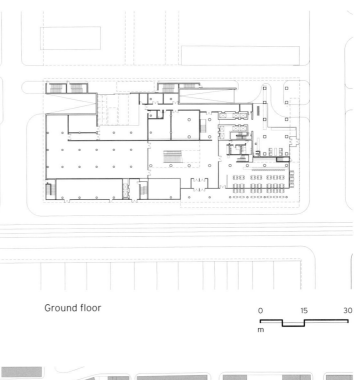

Ground floor

0   15   30
m

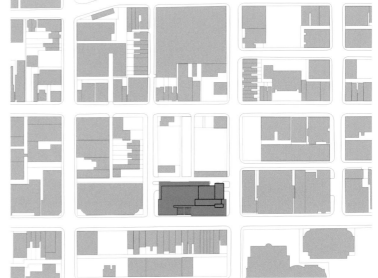

Vaughan Civic Centre
2010 VAUGHAN, ONTARIO

Originally a rural township located at the northern edge of Toronto,
the City of Vaughan is in the process of making the transition from
its rural past to an urban future. Since 1981, the town has grown from
29,647 to approximately 220,000 inhabitants, witnessing unprece-
dented growth and replacing farmland with housing and 'big box'
retail. The Vaughan Civic Centre is the winning scheme in an invited
design competition intended to set a tone for environmentally responsible and civic-minded development in the twenty-first century.

The competition terms required an architectural treatment for the
new City Hall building and a masterplan for the entire Civic Centre site,
which includes a diverse program of Civic Square, reference library,
Vaughan Hydro, a water feature, Chamber of Commerce, public gardens
and a heritage building. The solution — a campus of low-rise buildings
defining a public terrain of open spaces — was inspired by the clarity
of town planning in Ontario, where City Hall, Civic Square, market and
cenotaph form an identifiable civic precinct. In response to the city's
agricultural heritage, the campus is organized according to a series of
east-west bands informed by the linear patterns of local farmlands
as well as the larger framework of the concession grid. The buildings
are massed to step down in height from the north-east corner to the
lower pavilions located to the west and south. The City Hall and Civic
Tower anchor the composition and command the attention of approach-
ing traffic. The focal point of the Civic Square is the large reflecting
pool/skating rink. An allée of maple trees along the southern edge of
the Square leads to the main entrance of the City Hall.

The exterior cladding incorporates terra cotta, copper and glass
curtain wall, combined with thick slabs of Ontario Wiarton and Halton
Blue Ice stone for exterior landscape and interior floor finishes. Interior
spaces are finished in maple and stained walnut, and major public
circulation routes and assembly spaces will be finished in Ledgerock
and Ontario limestone.

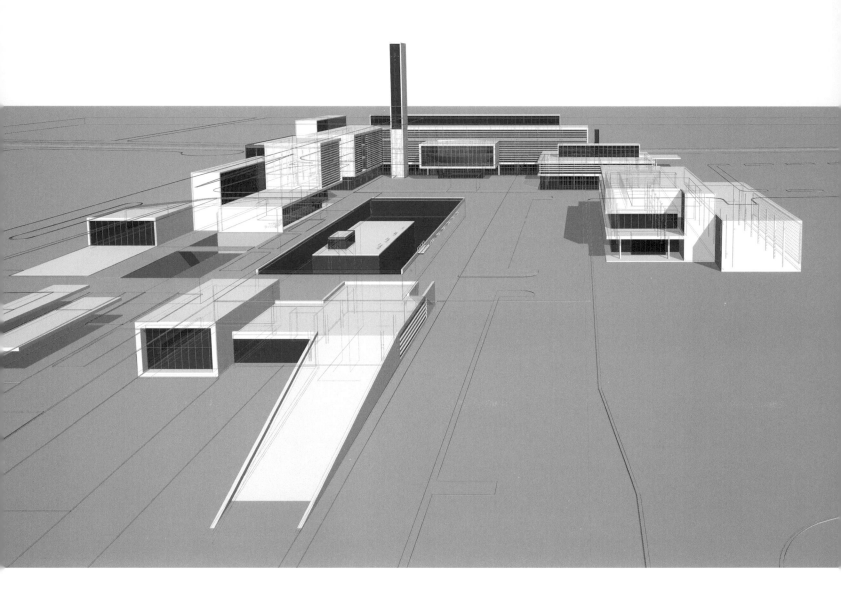

Project Chronology

Nicolas
1991 TORONTO

Kitchener City Hall
1993 KITCHENER, ONTARIO

Reisman-Jenkinson Residence
1991 RICHMOND HILL, ONTARIO

Ammirati Puris Lintas
1994 TORONTO

* indicates joint ventures (see page 203 for credits)

Marc Laurent
1986–91 TORONTO

King James Place
1991 TORONTO

Hasbro Headquarters
1994 PAWTUCKET, RHODE ISLAND

Dome Productions at the Skydome
1989 TORONTO

Woodsworth College,*
University of Toronto
1991 TORONTO

Design Exchange
1994 TORONTO

Tudhope Studios
1989 TORONTO

Creative Copy & Design
1992 TORONTO

Joseph S. Stauffer Library,
Queen's University
1994 KINGSTON, ONTARIO

35 East Wacker Drive
1990 CHICAGO

Oasis
1992 OAKVILLE, ONTARIO

Gluskin Sheff & Associates
1995 TORONTO

**Fields Institute for
Research in Advanced Mathematics**
1995 UNIVERSITY OF TORONTO

**Ettore Mazzoleni Concert Hall,
Royal Conservatory of Music**
1997 TORONTO

Indigo Books Music & More
1997 TORONTO, BURLINGTON AND
KINGSTON, ONTARIO

**Walter Carsen Centre for
National Ballet of Canada**
1996 TORONTO

Ammirati Puris Lintas
1997 NEW YORK

Disney Television Animation Studios
1997 TORONTO

Grand Valley Institution for Women
1996 KITCHENER-WATERLOO, ONTARIO

CIBC Wood Gundy
1997 TORONTO

McKee Public School
1998 NORTH YORK, ONTARIO

Alliance Communications
1996 TORONTO

Fort Lasalle Royal Military College
1997 KINGSTON, ONTARIO

Crabtree & Evelyn Flagship Stores
1998 PHILADELPHIA

Hummingbird Centre Phase 1
1996 TORONTO

Stratford Festival Theatre
1997 STRATFORD, ONTARIO

Chinese Cultural Centre*
1998 SCARBOROUGH, ONTARIO

Playdium@Sega City
1996 MISSISSAUGA, ONTARIO

Alias/wavefront
1997 TORONTO

Mitchell Field Community Centre
1998 NORTH YORK, ONTARIO

Hilton Airport Hotel
1998 TORONTO

Air Canada Club, Air Canada Centre
1999 TORONTO

Douglas Library, Queen's University
1999 KINGSTON, ONTARIO

500 Queen's Quay West
1999 TORONTO

Japanese Canadian Cultural Centre
2000 TORONTO

Hilton Toronto
2000 TORONTO

**Cardinal Ambrozic Houses
of Providence***
2000 SCARBOROUGH, ONTARIO

Richmond City Hall*
2000 RICHMOND, BRITISH COLUMBIA

**Munk Centre for International Studies,
University of Toronto**
2000 TORONTO

Penthouse on the Waterfront
2000 TORONTO

Goodman Theater*
2000 CHICAGO

Ravine House
2001 TORONTO

**Jackson-Triggs
Niagara Estate Winery**
2001 NIAGARA-ON-THE-LAKE, ONTARIO

Granite Club
2001 TORONTO

Star Alliance Lounge
2001 ZURICH INTERNATIONAL AIRPORT,
SWITZERLAND

Roy Thomson Hall Enhancement
2002 TORONTO

Central Park Lodge
2002 BURLINGTON AND RICHMOND HILL,
ONTARIO

**Genomics and Proteomics Research
Building, McGill University***
2003 MONTRÉAL

Raether Library and Information Technology Center, Trinity College
2003 HARTFORD, CONNECTICUT

James Stewart Centre for Mathematics, McMaster University
2003 HAMILTON, ONTARIO

St. Andrew's College
2003 AURORA, ONTARIO

Sprague Memorial Hall, Yale University
2003 NEW HAVEN, CONNECTICUT

Maple Leaf Lounge*
2004 TORONTO INTERNATIONAL AIRPORT

Centennial HP Science and Technology Centre, Centennial College*
2004 SCARBOROUGH, ONTARIO

Canadian Embassy*
2004 BERLIN, GERMANY

School of Management, University of Toronto
2004 SCARBOROUGH, ONTARIO

Le Quartier Concordia, Concordia University*
2005 MONTRÉAL

180 Queen Street West
2005 TORONTO

Art Gallery of Hamilton
2005 HAMILTON, ONTARIO

Gardiner Museum of Ceramic Art
2005 TORONTO

The National Ballet School*
2005 TORONTO

Royal Conservatory of Music Performance and Learning Centre
2005 TORONTO

Young Centre for the Performing Arts
2005 TORONTO

Canadian Museum of Nature*
2006 OTTAWA

Festival Centre and Tower, Toronto International Film Festival Group
2008 TORONTO

Vaughan Civic Centre
2010 VAUGHAN, ONTARIO

Project Credits

SELECTED WORK 1987–2004

Ammirati Puris Lintas
LOCATION: One Dag Hammarskjold Plaza, New York
COMPLETION DATE: May 1997
CLIENT: Ammirati Puris Lintas
PROGRAM: Phased renovation of 250,000 sq. ft. through 14 storeys of a 1970s high-rise office tower for open and closed workspaces, video conferencing, production and editing facilities, and conference and presentation rooms
CONTRACT VALUE: $27.2 million (US)
KPMB ARCHITECTS: Bruce Kuwabara (design partner); Shirley Blumberg (partner-in-charge); Kevin Mast and David Jesson (project architects); Anthony Provenzano, Heather Dubbeldam, Brian Main, Mike Poitras, Karen Petrachenko, Matthew Wilson, Mark Berest, Prish Jain, Leah Maguire (project team)
LOCAL ARCHITECT: John C. Fondrisi, AIA
ENGINEERS: Severud Associates (structural), Jaros Baum & Bolles Consulting Engineers (mechanical and electrical)
CONSULTANTS: Renee Cooley Lighting Design (lighting), Cosentini Associates (telecommunications), Barsky & Associates, Inc. (audio-visual), Cerami & Associates Inc. (acoustics)
GENERAL CONTRACTOR/CM: Structure Tone
PHOTOGRAPHS: Jeff Goldberg/ESTO, New York
SELECTED AWARDS: 1998 National Post Design Exchange Gold Award

Cardinal Ambrozic Houses of Providence
LOCATION: St. Clair and Warden Avenues adjacent to the Warden Woods Ravine, Scarborough, Ontario
COMPLETION DATE: May 2000
CLIENT: Providence Centre
PROGRAM: 212,000 sq. ft. new facility for 288 long-term care residents, sixteen 18-resident houses, including two Alzheimer units, Great Hall, chapel, retail, café
CONTRACT VALUE: $38 million
JOINT VENTURE ARCHITECTS: Montgomery and Sisam Architects, Kuwabara Payne McKenna Blumberg Architects, architects in joint venture for Providence Centre
KPMB ARCHITECTS: Marianne McKenna (partner-in-charge); Bruce Kuwabara (partner); Mitchell Hall (associate/project architect); John Allen (associate/contract administration); Andre D'Elia, John Wall, Rob Beraldo, Gianni Meogrossi, Leah Maguire, Paulo Rocha, Rob Kastelic, Karen Petrachenko, Kelly Buffey (project team)
MS ARCHITECTS: David Sisam (partner-in-charge), Terry Montgomery (partner); Robert Davies, Ed Applebaum (associates), Dave Smythe, Rob Smyth, David Lee, Santiago Kunzle
LANDSCAPE ARCHITECT: Vertechs Design
ENGINEERS: Read Jones Christoffersen Ltd. (structural), Crossey Engineering Ltd. (mechanical and electrical)
CONSULTANTS: Helyar & Associates (cost), Julie Bessant Pelech with Envirimed Inc. (programming), Judy Newcombe (furnishings), Marrack Watts (food services), Bhandari & Plater (signage)
PROJECT MANAGER: René Roy
GENERAL CONTRACTOR: Bondfield Construction
PHOTOGRAPHS: Steven Evans, Toronto (exteriors); Robert Burley Design Archive (interiors)
SELECTED AWARDS: 2000 National Post Design Exchange Gold Award; 2000 Toronto Architecture and Urban Design Award

Centennial HP Science and Technology Centre, Centennial College
LOCATION: Scarborough, Ontario
COMPLETION DATE: September 2004
CLIENT: Centennial College of Applied Arts and Technology
PROGRAM: 250,000 sq. ft. comprising classrooms, laboratories, lecture hall, resource centre, faculty offices, and food court/café
CONTRACT VALUE: $39.4 million
ASSOCIATED ARCHITECTS: Kuwabara Payne McKenna Blumberg Architects / Stone McQuire Vogt Architects, associated architects
KPMB ARCHITECTS: Bruce Kuwabara (design partner); Shirley Blumberg (partner-in-charge); Luigi LaRocca (senior associate); Paulo Rocha (project architect); Andre D'Elia, Ramon Janer, Shane O'Neill, Jimmy Sun, Steven Casey (project team)
SMV ARCHITECTS: Heinz Vogt (principal); Craig Bonham, Benny Domingos, Hassan Gardezi (project team)
LANDSCAPE ARCHITECT: NAK Design Group
ENGINEERS: Read Jones Christoffersen Ltd. (structural), Keen Engineering Co. Ltd. (mechanical), Mulvey & Banani International Inc. (electrical), Halsall Engineers (building envelope)
CONSULTANTS: Leber Rubes (life safety), IBI Group (IT), ITRANS Consulting Inc. (traffic), Urban Watershed Group (stormwater management), Decommissioning Consulting Services Ltd. (geotechnical), Entro Communications (signage)
CONSTRUCTION MANAGER: Vanbots Construction Corporation
PHOTOGRAPHS: Tom Arban Photography, Toronto

Design Exchange
LOCATION: 234 Bay Street, Toronto, Ontario
COMPLETION DATE: September 1994
CLIENT: Design Exchange
PROGRAM: 40,000 sq. ft. of exhibition space, resource centre, café, members lounge, retail store, administrative offices, and multi-purpose seminar rooms
CONTRACT VALUE: $4.5 million
KPMB ARCHITECTS: Shirley Blumberg (partner-in-charge); Bruce Kuwabara (partner); Siamak Hariri (associate); Todd Macyk (project architect); David Jesson, Karen Petrachenko, Kelly Lem, Mike Poitras, Anthony Provenzano (project team)
ENGINEERS: Yolles Partnership Ltd. (structural), Merber Corporation (mechanical), Carinci Burt Rogers Engineering (electrical), Morrison Hershfield Ltd (fire and life safety)
CONSULTANTS: Brian Arnott Associates (audio-visual), Paul Mathiesen Light & Design, Valcoustics Canada Ltd. (acoustics), James F. Vermeulen Cost Consultant Ltd. (cost), Morrison Hershfield (life safety), Donald Kaufman (colour), Gottschalk & Ash (signage)
PROJECT MANAGER: Alan Dudeck
GENERAL CONTRACTOR: The Jackson-Lewis Company, Limited

PHOTOGRAPHS: Robert Burley/Design Archive;
Steven Evans, Toronto
SELECTED AWARDS: 1997 Governor General's Award;
1995 Toronto Historical Board Award; 1995
Architectural Record Interiors Award of
Excellence

Dome Productions at the Skydome

LOCATION: Toronto, Ontario
COMPLETION DATE: June 1989:
CLIENT: Dome Productions
PROGRAM: 20,000 sq. ft. live broadcast/ post-production
facility
CONTRACT VALUE: $4 million plus $15 million for furnish-
ings, fittings and equipment
KPMB ARCHITECTS: Bruce Kuwabara (partner-in-charge);
Luigi LaRocca (project architect); Howard Sutcliffe,
Lexi Kolt-Wagner, Steven Robinson, Jason King
(project team)
ENGINEERS: M.S. Yolles & Partners (structural),
Merber Corporation (mechanical), Carinci Burt
Rogers Engineering (electrical), Valcoustics
Canada Ltd. (acoustics), Leber-Rubes Inc. (fire
and life safety)
CONSULTANTS: Centro Corporation (communication
engineer)
CONSTRUCTION MANAGEMENT: Dalton Engineering and
Construction Ltd.
PHOTOGRAPHS: Steven Evans, Toronto
SELECTED AWARDS: 1990 Millimeter Magazine Award
for Best Facility Planning and Design Achievement
in North America

Genomics and Proteomics Research Building, McGill University

LOCATION: 740 Docteur Penfield, McGill University,
Montréal, Québec
COMPLETION DATE: January 2003
CLIENT: McGill University
PROGRAM: 92,000 sq. ft. of research laboratories, offices,
and commercial incubator space
CONTRACT VALUE: $20 million
JOINT VENTURE ARCHITECTS: Kuwabara Payne McKenna
Blumberg Architects / Fichten Soiferman et Associés,
Architectes, architects in joint venture
KPMB ARCHITECTS: Marianne McKenna (partner-in-
charge); Mitchell Hall (associate and project design
architect); Robert Kastelic, Brent Wagler, Eric Ho,
Christine Levine, Jill Osiowy, Lheila Palumbo,
Chris Wegner (project team)
FSA ARCHITECTS: Jacob Fichten (managing architect),
Robert Lacoste (production architect), Bernard

Jacques, Julie Dionne, Martine Lacombe, Michael
Conway, Benoit Lamoureux, Annie-Claude Sauvé,
Benoit Picard (project team)
ENGINEERS: Saia Deslauriers Kadanoff LeConte Brisebois
Blais (structural), Pellemon Inc. (mechanical and
electrical), Vinci Consultants (civil)
CONSULTANTS: Civilec Consultants Inc. (code), Michael
Shapiro (users representative)
PROJECT MANAGER: Le Group Décarel Inc.
GENERAL CONTRACTOR: J.E. Verreault et Fils Ltée
DIGITAL RENDERING: Rob Kastelic, Toronto
PHOTOGRAPHS: Michel Brunelle, Montréal; Eduard
Hueber, Arch Photo Inc., New York

Goodman Theater

LOCATION: 170 North Dearborn Street, Chicago, Illinois
COMPLETION DATE: 2000
CLIENT: The Goodman Theater
PROGRAMS: New 800-seat theatre building, renovation
of two existing theatre buildings to accommodate
administrative, backstage and rehearsal facilities,
and a 400-seat repertory theatre
CONTRACT VALUE: $32.5 million (US)
ASSOCIATED ARCHITECTS: Kuwabara Payne McKenna
Blumberg Architects, DLK Architecture Inc.,
McClier Corporation, associated architects for
The Goodman Theater
KPMB ARCHITECTS: Thomas Payne (partner-in-charge);
Chris Couse (senior associate); Goran Milosevic
(associate); Mark Jaffar (project architect); David
Poloway, Andre D'Elia, Jason Pearson (project team)
DLK ARCHITECTS: Howard Decker, Diane Legge Kemp, Hill
Burgess, Behrnt Aaberg
ENGINEERS: TT-CBM Engineers with Salse Engineering
Associates (structural), Environmental Systems
Design Inc. with Globetrotters Engineering Corp.
(mechanical and electrical), Rolf Jensen &
Associates (fire and life safety), Schuler and
Shook Inc. (lighting)
CONSULTANTS: Theatre Projects Consultants (theatre),
The Talaske Group (acoustics and noise control),
McClier Corporation (consulting architect—
terra cotta restoration)
PHOTOGRAPHS: Jeff Goldberg/ESTO, New York

Grand Valley Institution for Women

LOCATION: Kitchener, Ontario
COMPLETION DATE: June 1996
CLIENT: Public Works Canada and Correctional
Services Canada
PROGRAM: 74,536 sq. ft. (main building and
10 residential units)

CONTRACT VALUE: $9.4 million
KPMB ARCHITECTS: Marianne McKenna (partner-in-
charge); Bruce Kuwabara (partner); Robert Sims
(project architect); Howard Sutcliffe, David
Pontarini, John Allen, Lexi Kolt-Wagner, Jeff Wagner,
Karen Petrachenko (project team)
LANDSCAPE ARCHITECT: Milus Bollenberghe Topps
Watchorn
ENGINEERS: Read Jones Christoffersen Ltd. (structural),
Crossey Engineering Ltd. (mechanical and electrical),
Conestoga Rovers & Associates (civil)
COST CONSULTANT: James F. Vermeulen Inc.
GENERAL CONTRACTOR: G.W. Harkness Contracting Ltd.
PHOTOGRAPHS: Steven Evans, Toronto; Peter Gill,
Toronto
SELECTED AWARDS: 1997 Governor General's Award;
1997 American Institute of Architects' Certificate
of Merit

Hilton Toronto, Toronto

LOCATION: 145 Richmond Street West, Toronto, Ontario
COMPLETION DATE: Phase 1: April 1998 (300 guest rooms,
meeting room floor); Phase 2: April 2000 (300 guest
rooms, public areas)
CLIENT: Hilton (Canada) / London & Leeds Development
Corporation
PROGRAM: 292,582 sq. ft. of phased renovations to exist-
ing public areas (entrance court, lobby, mezzanine,
meeting rooms), 27 floors and 600 guest rooms
CONTRACT VALUE: $17 million
KPMB ARCHITECTS: Thomas Payne (partner-in-charge);
David Jesson, Victoria Gregory (associates);
Greg Guerra, Robert Kastelic, Kelly Chow, Paulo
Rocha, Bill Colaco, Ulrike Lubeck, Miyako Panalaks,
Tom Strickland, Annette Lee; Interior Designers:
Karen Petrachenko, Kelly Buffey, Jill Osiowy,
Carolyn Lee (project team)
ENGINEERS: Yolles Partnership Ltd. (structural),
Maunder Britnell Inc. (mechanical and electrical)
CONSULTANTS: II by IV Design Associates Inc. (interior
design—Tundra restaurant), George Sexton
Associates (lighting), Leber Rubes (code), Sacom
Associates (fire and life safety)
GENERAL CONTRACTOR: Pantar Developments Inc.
PHOTOGRAPHS: Peter Sellar/KLIK; Volker Seding, Toronto;
David Whittaker, Toronto.
SELECTED AWARDS: 2001 Interior Design Hospitality
Award, Best Renovation; 2001 Canadian Interiors
Best of Canada Design Competition, Project
Winner; 2000 National Post Design Exchange
Gold Award

Jackson-Triggs Niagara Estate Winery

LOCATION: 2145 Regional Road 55, Niagara-on-the-Lake, Ontario

COMPLETION DATE: July 2001

CLIENT: Vincor International Inc.

PROGRAM: 43,000 sq. ft. winery

KPMB ARCHITECTS: Marianne McKenna (partner-in-charge); Bruce Kuwabara (partner); Mitchell Hall (associate/project architect); Glenn MacMullin, Andre D'Elia, Chris Beamer, Rob Beraldo, Gianni Meogrossi, Deni DiFilippo, Christine Levine, Rufina Wu, Katie Triggs, Karen Petrachenko, Jill Osiowy (project team)

LANDSCAPE ARCHITECT: Janet Rosenberg & Associates

ENGINEERS: Blackwell Engineering Ltd. (structural), Keen Engineering Co. Ltd. (mechanical), Carinci Burt Rogers Engineering, Inc.(electrical), Kerry T. Howe Engineering (civil)

CONSULTANTS: Agra Earth & Environmental (soils), Vermeulens Cost Consultants (cost), Marrack & Associates Inc. (food services), Bhandari & Plater Inc. (signage), Engineering Concepts Niagara (process), Design Electronics (audio visual), Suzanne Powadiuk Design Inc. (lighting)

CONSTRUCTION MANAGER: Merit Contractors of Niagara

TRADES: Millworks Custom Fabricators (special fixtures, furniture)

PHOTOGRAPHS: Robert Burley/Design Archive; Peter Sellar/KLIK; Eduard Hueber, Arch Photo Inc., New York; Peter Wagner, Skylab Media, Toronto

SELECTED AWARDS: 2003 National Post Design Exchange Award, Environments; 2003 Business Week/Architectural Record Award, Finalist; 2002 Ontario Association of Architects' Architectural Excellence Award; 2002 Interior Design Hospitality Award; 1999 Canadian Architect Award of Excellence

James Stewart Centre for Mathematics, McMaster University

LOCATION: Hamilton, Ontario

COMPLETION DATE: September 2003

CLIENT: McMaster University

PROGRAM: 49,000 sq. ft. interior adaptive reuse, including classrooms, faculty offices, math laboratories, graduate study areas and café

CONTRACT VALUE: $8.5 million

KPMB ARCHITECTS: Bruce Kuwabara (design partner); Shirley Blumberg (partner-in-charge); Luigi LaRocca (senior associate); Kevin Bridgman (project architect); Bruno Weber, Garth Zimmer, Simon Haus (project team); Katya Marshall, Dianna Liu

ENGINEERS: Stantec Consulting Ltd. (structural, mechanical and electrical), Halsall Associates Ltd. (building envelope), Leber-Rubes Inc. (fire and life safety)

CONSULTANTS: Curran McCabe Ravindran Ross (cost), Pinchin Environmental (environmental)

PROJECT MANAGER: O.P. McCarthy & Associates

GENERAL CONTRACTOR: Alberici Constructors Ltd.

PHOTOGRAPHS: Eduard Hueber, Arch Photo Inc., New York; Tom Arban Photography, Toronto

SELECTED AWARDS: 2004 Governor General's Medal

Japanese Canadian Cultural Centre

LOCATION: 6 Garamond Court, Don Mills, Ontario

COMPLETION DATE: Phase 1: March 2000; Phase 2: 2004

CLIENT: Japanese Canadian Cultural Centre

PROGRAM: Phase 1 (33,000 sq. ft.): Shokokai Court, Gendai Gallery, martial arts centre, multi-purpose spaces for cultural and education programs; Phase 2 (22,500 sq. ft.): Auditorium, heritage lounge, multi-purpose program spaces

CONTRACT VALUE: Phase 1: $2.5 million; Phase 2: $3.15 million

KPMB ARCHITECTS: Bruce Kuwabara (design partner); Shirley Blumberg (partner-in-charge); Phase 1: Robert Sims (associate); Karen Cvornyek, Matthew Wilson, Paulo Rocha, Gianni Meogrossi, Miyako Panalaks (project team); Phase 2: Safdar Abidi, Anne Lok, Bill Colaco (project team)

ENGINEERS: Yolles Partnership Ltd (structural and building envelope), Crossey Engineering Ltd. (mechanical and electrical) (Phase 1); Yolles Partnership Ltd. (structural), Merber Corporation (mechanical and electrical) (Phase 2)

CONSULTANTS: Briggs Environmental Canada Ltd. (environmental), Brian Arnott Associates (theatre), Vermeulens Cost Consultants (cost) (Phase 1); Novita (theatre), Aercoustics (acoustical), Vermeulens Cost Consultants (cost) (Phase 2)

PHOTOGRAPHS: Volker Seding, Toronto

Joseph S. Stauffer Library, Queen's University

LOCATION: Queen's University, Kingston, Ontario

COMPLETION DATE: October 1994

CLIENT: Queen's University

PROGRAM: 230,000 sq. ft. library and computing centre

CONTRACT VALUE: $37.5 million

KPMB ARCHITECTS: Thomas Payne (partner-in-charge); Christopher Couse, David Pontarini (associates); Judith Taylor, Victoria Gregory, Goran Milosevic (project architects); Alan Vihant, Andrew Dyke, Robert Sims, Robert Gilvesy, Katherine Pankrantz, Fred Allin, Lexi Kolt-Wagner (project team)

CONSULTING ARCHITECTS: Moffat Kinoshita Associates Inc. (contract documents phase)

ENGINEERS: Halsall Associates Limited (structural and building science), JSA Energy Analysts (mechanical), Mulvey & Banani International Inc. (electrical)

CONSULTANTS: Vermeulens Cost Consultants (cost), Ferris & Quinn Associates Inc. (landscape), McAdams Planning Consultants (library), Leber-Rubes Inc. (fire and life safety)

GENERAL CONTRACTOR: Eastern Construction Company

PHOTOGRAPHS: Steven Evans, Toronto; Jeff Goldberg/ESTO, New York

SELECTED AWARDS: 2001 City of Kingston Livable City Design Award; 1997 Governor General's Award

King James Place

LOCATION: King Street East, Toronto

COMPLETION DATE: December 1991

CLIENT: Equifund Corporation

PROGRAM: 55,000 sq. ft. of commercial office; 8,500 sq. ft. of retail at grade

CONTRACT VALUE: $7 million

KPMB ARCHITECTS: Shirley Blumberg (partner-in-charge); Bruce Kuwabara (design partner); Michael Taylor (associate); Byron Carter, Michael Poitras, Josef Neuwirth, Elaine Didyk (project team)

ENGINEERS: Read Jones Christoffersen Ltd. (structural), Merber Corporation (mechanical), Carinci Burt Rogers Engineering (electrical)

PHOTOGRAPHS: Steven Evans, Toronto

SELECTED AWARDS: 1994 Toronto Historical Board Award; 1992 Governor General's Award; 1992 Toronto Masonry Award, Overall Winner

Kitchener City Hall

LOCATION: 200 King Street West, Kitchener, Ontario

COMPETITION DATE: 1989

COMPLETION DATE: September 1993

CLIENT: City of Kitchener

PROGRAM: Program 200,000 sq. ft. above ground; 200,000 sq. ft. below grade parking

CONTRACT VALUE: $43.4 million

COMPETITION TEAM: Bruce Kuwabara, Howard Sutcliffe, Matthew Wilson, Mark Jaffar, Andrew Dyke, John Czechowsky

KPMB ARCHITECTS: Bruce Kuwabara (partner-in-charge); Marianne McKenna (partner); Luigi LaRocca (associate); Howard Sutcliffe, David Pontarini, Judith Taylor, Andrew Dyke, Mitchell Hall, Evan Webber, Bill Colaco, Mark Jaffar, Matthew Wilson, John Allen, Kevin Mast, Jill Calvert,

Karen Petrachenko, John Cook, Joseph Neuwirth, Glenn MacMullin, Larry Chow, Michael Poitras, Birgit Siber (project team)
LANDSCAPE ARCHITECT: Milus Bollenberghe Topps Watchorn
ENGINEERS: Yolles Partnership Ltd. (structural), Merber Corporation (mechanical), Mulvey & Banani International Inc. (electrical), Leber-Rubes Inc. (fire and life safety)
CONSULTANTS: James F. Vermeulen Cost Consultant Ltd. (cost), Rice Brydone Ltd. (office interiors), Tudhope Associates (signage and graphics), Ken Lewis (A/V)
GENERAL CONTRACTOR: Ellis-Don Construction
PHOTOGRAPHS: Eduard Hueber, Arch Photo Inc., New York; Steven Evans, Toronto; Robert Hill, Toronto; Michael Awad, Toronto
SELECTED AWARDS: 1994 Governor General's Medal for Excellence; 1990 Canadian Architect Award of Excellence

Lexus Lounge, Roy Thomson Hall
LOCATION: Toronto, Ontario
COMPLETION DATE: 2004
CLIENT: The Corporation of Massey Hall and Roy Thomson Hall
PROGRAMS: Transformation of existing rehearsal hall into patron's lounge and meeting space
CONTRACT VALUE: withheld at client's request
KPMB ARCHITECTS: Thomas Payne (partner-in-charge); David Jesson (associate); Nicolas Choy, John Agnidis (project team); Karen Petrachenko (interior designer)
ENGINEERS: Carruthers & Wallace Ltd. (structural), The Mitchell Partnership Inc. (mechanical), Carinci Burt Rogers Engineering Inc. (electrical), Leber Rubes Inc. (fire and life safety)
CONSULTANTS: Suzanne Powadiuk (lighting)
CONSTRUCTION MANAGER: Dalton Engineering & Construction Limited
PHOTOGRAPHS: Peter Sellar/KLIK

Marc Laurent
LOCATION: Toronto, Ontario
COMPLETION DATE: Four phases completed between 1986–1991
CLIENT: Henry Bendayan
PROGRAM: 7,000 sq. ft. retail store
CONTRACT VALUE: Withheld at client's request
KPMB ARCHITECTS: Bruce Kuwabara, Thomas Payne (partners-in-charge); Lexi Kolt-Wagner, Larry Chow, Jason King, Todd Macyk (project team)

ENGINEERS: Merber Corporation (mechanical and electrical)
PHOTOGRAPHS: Steven Evans, Toronto (Phase I and II)
SELECTED AWARDS: 1990–91 Ontario Association of Architects' Architectural Excellence Award

Raether Library and Information Technology Center, Trinity College
LOCATION: Hartford, Connecticut
COMPLETION DATE: July 2003
CLIENT: Trinity College
PROGRAM: 118,000 sq. ft. renovation of two buildings: the original 1952 building and a 1977 addition, 62,000 sq. ft. of new construction
CONTRACT VALUE: $26 million (US)
KPMB ARCHITECTS: Thomas Payne (partner-in-charge); Goran Milosevic, Victoria Gregory (associates); Margaret Graham, Mark Jaffar, Alex Lam, Brent Wagler, Matthew Wilson, Ramon Janer, Nelson Kwong, Katya Marshall, Bill Colaco, Jill Osiowy (project team)
LANDSCAPE ARCHITECT: Sasaki Associates Inc.
ENGINEERS: Le Messurier Consultants (structural), VanZelm Heywood & Shadford Inc. (mechanical and electrical), Westcott and Mapes, Inc. (civil), Philip R. Sherman (fire and life safety, R.J. Kenney Associates, Inc. (building envelope)
CONSULTANTS: Suzanne Powadiuk Designs (lighting), Ducibella Venter & Santore (security), Vermeulens Cost Consultants (cost), Haley & Aldrich Inc. (geotechnical)
CONSTRUCTION MANAGER: Gilbane Construction Company
PROGRAM MANAGER: Trammell Crow Company
PHOTOGRAPHS: Jeff Goldberg/ESTO; Peter Sellar/KLIK; Al Ferreira, Photography, Hartford, Connecticut

Ravine House
LOCATION: Toronto, Ontario
COMPLETION DATE: January 2001
CLIENT: Withheld at owner's request
PROGRAM: 11,000 sq. ft. residence
KPMB ARCHITECTS: Bruce Kuwabara (partner-in-charge); Kevin Bridgman, Paulo Rocha (project architects); Karen Petrachenko, Kelly Buffey (furnishings)
LANDSCAPE DESIGN: KPMB Architects, NAK Design (plantings), Cornelia Hahn Oberlander (special consulting)
ENGINEERS: Yolles Partnership Inc. (structural), Merber Corporation (mechanical and electrical)
CONSULTANTS: Suzanne Powadiuk Designs (lighting)
GENERAL CONTRACTOR: Eisner | Murray Developments Ltd., Steven Eisner

SITE SUPERINTENDENT: Vic Furgiuele
TRADES: Millwork: Gregory Rybak, Richard Dubicki, Jurek Galinski
PHOTOGRAPHS: Walter Mair, Zurich; Steven Evans, Toronto; Peter Sellar/KLIK; Eduard Hueber, Arch Photo Inc., New York
SELECTED AWARDS: 2003 Ontario Association of Architects' Annual Awards — Single Family Residence Award

Reisman-Jenkinson Residence
LOCATION: Richmond Hill, Ontario
COMPLETION DATE: Spring 1991
CLIENT: Steven Jenkinson and Dolly Reisman
PROGRAM: 3,800 sq. ft. incorporating sculpture studio, writing studio, entrance conservatory, bedrooms, kitchen, living and dining rooms
CONTRACT VALUE: $550,000
KPMB ARCHITECTS: Bruce Kuwabara (partner-in-charge); Evan Webber (project architect)
ENGINEERS: Yolles Partnership Ltd. (structural), Michel Perrault (building envelope)
GENERAL CONTRACTOR: Lora Lane Group Inc.
PHOTOGRAPHS: Steven Evans, Toronto
SELECTED AWARDS: 1994 Governor General's Award

Richmond City Hall
LOCATION: 6911 No. 3 Road, Richmond, British Columbia
COMPETITION DATE: October 1997
COMPLETION DATE: May 2000
CLIENT: City of Richmond
PROGRAM: 119,662 sq. ft. above grade; 81,970 sq. ft. below grade
CONTRACT VALUE: $30 million
ASSOCIATED ARCHITECTS: Hotson Bakker Architects / Kuwabara Payne McKenna Blumberg Architects, associated architects for Richmond City Hall
KPMB ARCHITECTS: Bruce Kuwabara (partner-in-charge); Judith Taylor (associate); Andre D'Elia, John Wall, Glenn MacMullin (project architects); Bill Colaco, Neil Bauman, Riki Nishimura (project team)
HOTSON BAKKER ARCHITECTS: Joost Bakker (principal-in-charge); Joyce Drohan (project architect); Rick Clarke, Kate Gerson, Andreas Kaminsky, Scott Edwards, Deryk Whitehead (project team)
LANDSCAPE ARCHITECT: Phillips Farevaag Smallenberg Inc.
ENGINEERS: Bush Bohman & Partners (structural), DWT Stanley with Tescor Pacific Energy Services (mechanical), R.A. Duff & Associates (electrical)
CONSULTANTS: Locke MacKinnon Domingo Gibson & Associates Ltd. (fire and life safety), Barron Kennedy Lyzun & Associates Ltd. (acoustics)

PROJECT MANAGER: Dominion Construction (Project and Construction Managers)

GENERAL CONTRACTOR: Dominion Construction

PHOTOGRAPHS: Martin Tessler, Vancouver; Peter Aaron/ESTO; Chris Phillips, Vancouver

SELECTED AWARDS: 2002 Governor General's Medal; 2001 Lieutenant Governor of British Columbia Merit Award

Roy Thomson Hall Enhancement

LOCATION: 60 Simcoe Street, Toronto, Ontario

COMPLETION DATE: September 2002

CLIENT: The Corporation of Massey Hall and Roy Thomson Hall

PROGRAM: Transformation of the stage and auditorium chamber (60,000 sq. ft.) to create a room with great natural acoustics

CONTRACT VALUE: $15 million

KPMB ARCHITECTS: Thomas Payne (partner-in-charge); Christopher Couse (senior associate); David Jesson (associate); John Agnidis, Athos Zaghi, Rob Kastelic, Franziska Cape, Simon Haus, Shadi Rahbaran, Brian Urbanik, Graham Ferrier, Chris Lyle, Denis DiFilippo, Carolyn Lee (project team), Karen Petrachenko (interior designer)

ENGINEERS: Artec Consultants Inc. (acoustics and noise control and theatre consulting), Carruthers and Wallace Limited (structural), The Mitchell Partnership Inc. (mechanical), Mulvey and Banani International Inc. (electrical)

CONSULTANTS: Artec Consultants Inc. (acoustics, theatre, performance lighting consultants), Steve A. Walker (theatrical rigging), Suzanne Powadiuk (architectural lighting), Leber/Rubes (fire and life safety)

GENERAL CONTRACTOR: Ellis-Don Construction

SPECIAL TRADES: JOEL Theatrical (Rigging)

PHOTOGRAPHS: Peter Sellar/KLIK; William Conley, Toronto (construction photos)

Sprague Memorial Hall, Yale University

LOCATION: New Haven, Connecticut

COMPLETION DATE: August 2003

CLIENT: Yale University, School of Music

PROGRAM: 34,000 sq. ft. renovation and additions to the 1917 Coolidge & Shattuck building, including rejuvenation of the existing 720-seat recital hall, new MEP systems, and new administrative and practice facilities

CONTRACT VALUE: $16 million (US)

KPMB ARCHITECTS: Thomas Payne (partner-in-charge); Christopher Couse (senior associate); David

Poloway (project architect); Judith Taylor, Margaret Graham, Aaron Letki, Jill Osiowy (project team)

CONSULTING ARCHITECT: Patrick Pinnell Architect

LANDSCAPE ARCHITECT: Towers/ Golde with Cornelia Hahn Oberlander

ENGINEERS: LZA/Thornton Tomasetti Engineers (structural), Altieri Sebor Wieber LLC (MEP/FP)

CONSULTANTS: R. Lawrence Kirkegaard and Associates (acoustics), George Sexton Associates (lighting), Theatre Projects Consultants (performance lighting); Vermeulens Cost Consultant (cost), Bruce J. Spiewak (fire and life safety)

GENERAL CONTRACTOR: Turner Construction

PHOTOGRAPHS: Jeff Goldberg/ESTO, New York

SELECTED AWARDS: 2004 USITT Merit Award

Star Alliance Lounge

LOCATION: Terminal B, Zurich International Airport, Switzerland

COMPETITION DATE: September 2000

COMPLETION DATE: July 2001

CLIENT: Star Alliance

PROGRAM: 7,700 sq. ft. airport lounge

CONTRACT VALUE: Withheld at client's request

COMPETITION TEAM: Bruce Kuwabara; Paolo Rocha; Dan Nawrocki, Chris Lyle (renderings)

KPMB ARCHITECTS: Bruce Kuwabara (partner-in-charge); Luigi LaRocca (senior associate); Paulo Rocha, Bruno Weber (project architects); Kevin Bridgman, Valerie Gow, Karen Petrachenko, Carolyn Lee (project team)

LOCAL ARCHITECT: Liz Etzold Architektin (Zurich)

ENGINEERS: Bakoplan Elektro Ingenieure (electrical), Biasca Engineering (mechanical)

CONSULTANTS: Liz Etzold Architektin (local architect, Zurich); Vermeulens Cost Consultants (cost); LSG Sky Chefs (food services, Zurich); Hans Besser, Lufthansa German Airlines, Pentagram (signage and graphics); Gamma AG (stone); Leicht Metall Ban AG (metal); Paul Kleger AG (wood); Phonex-Gema AG (metal mesh); Lenzhinger Söhne AG (wood floor & carpet); Nenco AG (lighting); B&B Italia, Cappellini, Cassina, Vitra, Flexform, Alias (furniture)

PROJECT MANAGER: James Donaldson Architect

CONSTRUCTION MANAGER: Halter Generalunternehmung AG

PHOTOGRAPHS : Walter Mair, Zurich; Ted Fahn, Copenhagen

St. Andrew's College

LOCATION: 100-acre St. Andrew's College campus, Aurora, Ontario

COMPLETION DATE: 2003

CLIENT: St. Andrew's College

PROGRAM: 35,700 sq. ft. middle school; 9,900 sq. ft. gallery; 7,900 sq. ft. arts centre (total: 53,500 sq. ft.)

CONTRACT VALUE: $12 million (phased construction)

KPMB ARCHITECTS: Marianne McKenna (partner-in-charge); Robert Sims (associate); David Smythe (project architect); Christine Levine, Simon Haus, Katya Marshall, Andrew Butler, Andrea Kordos, Carolyn Lee, Clare Radford, Bill Colaco (project team)

LANDSCAPE ARCHITECT: Janet Rosenberg & Associates Inc.

ENGINEERS: Read Jones Christoffersen (structural), Smith and Andersen (mechanical), Carinci Burt Rogers (electrical), Cansult (civil)

CONSULTANTS: Curran McCabe Ravindran Ross Inc. (cost), Leber-Rubes Inc. (building code), Wespec (specifications), Suzanne Powadiuk (lighting)

PROJECT MANAGER: PHA Project Management Inc., Paul Hatton, Ron Barry

GENERAL CONTRACTOR: Eastern Construction Company Ltd.

SPECIAL TRADES: MCM 2001 (special fixtures, custom light fixtures)

MODEL: JS Models

PHOTOGRAPHS: Eduard Hueber, Arch Photo Inc., New York

Tudhope Studios

LOCATION: 284 King Street East, Toronto, Ontario

COMPLETION DATE: 1989

CLIENT: Tudhope Associates

PROGRAM: 12,000 sq. ft. in 2 phases, comprising design studios, production areas, offices, conference rooms and kitchen; 4,000 sq. ft. retail showroom

CONTRACT VALUE: $1.2 million

KPMB ARCHITECTS: Marianne McKenna, Bruce Kuwabara (partners-in-charge); Howard Sutcliffe, Luigi LaRocca, Beverley Horii, Neil Morfitt (project team)

ENGINEERS: M.S. Yolles & Partners (structural), Merber Corporation (mechanical), Carinci Burt Rogers Engineering (electrical)

CONSULTANTS: Suzanne Powadiuk Designs (lighting), Dynamix Professional Video Consultants (A/V)

GENERAL CONTRACTOR: Phase 1: J.D. Strachan

SPECIAL TRADES: Millworks Custom Fabricators Inc. (special furniture) Expo Iron Works Ltd. (metal)

PHOTOGRAPHS: Estate of Wolfgang Hoyt/ESTO; Steven Evans, Toronto

Woodsworth College, University of Toronto

LOCATION: Toronto, Ontario

COMPLETION DATE: December 1991

CLIENT: Woodsworth College, University of Toronto

PROGRAM: 19,840 sq. ft. new construction (classrooms, faculty offices, and communal facilities); 21,800 sq. ft. renovation of three historic houses and existing Drill Hall examination facilities

CONTRACT VALUE: $8 million

ARCHITECTS: Barton Myers Architect Inc. / Kuwabara Payne McKenna Blumberg Architects, associated architects

KPMB ARCHITECTS: Thomas Payne (partner-in-charge); Siamak Hariri (associate); Victoria Gregory, David Pontarini, Howard Sutcliffe; Andrew Blackwell, John Cook, Joseph Neuwirth, Mitchell Hall, Robert Sims, Birgit Siber, Goran Milosevic, Rob Gilvesy (project team)

BARTON MYERS ARCHITECT: Barton Myers

LANDSCAPE ARCHITECT: Ferris McCluskey Quinn & Associates

ENGINEERS: Yolles Partnership Ltd. (structural), Merber Corporation (mechanical and electrical), J.C. Perrault & Sons (building envelope)

COST CONSULTANTS: A.J. Vermeulen Inc., Leber-Rubes Inc. (fire and life safety)

GENERAL CONTRACTOR: Jaltas Inc.

PHOTOGRAPHS: Steven Evans, Toronto

SELECTED AWARDS: 1995 City of Toronto Urban Design Award; 1993 AIA Brick in Architecture Award; 1992–93 OAA Architectural Excellence Award; 1992 Governor General's Medal for Excellence

WORK IN PROGRESS

Canadian Embassy, Berlin, Germany

LOCATION: South of the Brandenburg Gate and Reichstag at Ebertstrasse and Leipziger Platz, Berlin, Germany

COMPETITION DATE: 1998

COMPLETION DATE: Fall 2004

CLIENT: Government of Canada, Department of Foreign Affairs and International Trade

PROGRAM: 160,000 sq. ft., including the new Canadian embassy, the Department of Foreign Affairs and International Trade, public, commercial and residential space

JOINT VENTURE ARCHITECTS: Kuwabara Payne McKenna Blumberg Architects, Gagnon Letellier Cyr, architectes, and Smith Carter Architects + Engineers Inc., architects in joint venture

COMPETITION TEAM: Bruce Kuwabara, James Yamashita, Marc Letellier, Cornelia Oberlander; Simon Brochu, Andrew Dyke, Mitchell Hall, Chris Lyle, Riki Nishimura, Barbara Vogel, Jacek Vogel, Takashi Yamashita

KPMB ARCHITECTS: Bruce Kuwabara (partner-in-charge); Luigi LaRocca (senior associate); Andrew Dyke (associate); Bill Colaco, Deni Di Filippo, Brian Graham, Simon Haus, Robert Kastelic, Riki Nishimura, Shadi Rahbaran, Bruno Weber, Franciska Cape, Karen Petrachenko, Carolyn Lee, Dan Nawrocki (project team)

GAGNON LETELLIER CYR, ARCHITECTES: Marc Letellier, Michel Gagnon (senior architects); Simon Brochu, Jean-Sébastien Laberge (architects), Pierre Michaud, Réal St-Pierre, Guylaine Lehoux (technologists)

SMITH CARTER ARCHITECTS AND ENGINEERS INCORPORATED: James Yamashita (project management); Takashi Yamashita (A/E integration); Colin Gibbs (structural engineering); Jim McEwen, Gary Hornby (mechanical engineering); Howard Procyshyn, Steven Smart (electrical engineering)

LOCAL ARCHITECT: Pysall Ruge von Matt Architekten (local executive architect—Berlin), RAVE Architekten (local consulting architect—Berlin)

LANDSCAPE ARCHITECT: Cornelia Hahn Oberlander

ENGINEERS: GSE Ingenieur-Gesellschaft mbH Saar, Enseleit und Partner (structural), Happold Ingenieurbüro GmbH (mechanical and electrical)

CONSULTANTS: Vogel Architects (office interiors), Suzanne Powadiuk Design (lighting), Vermeulens Cost Consultants (cost)

DEVELOPER: Hannover Leasing, Tercon Immobilien

GENERAL CONTRACTOR: Alpine EBan

SPECIAL TRADES: Steelwork (glass & glazing) Vetter (stone)

3-D MODELS: Buenck + Fehse, Berlin

PHOTOGRAPHY: Ben Rahn / A Frame, Toronto

Festival Centre and Tower, Toronto International Film Festival Group

LOCATION: Northwest corner of King and John Streets, Toronto, Ontario

COMPETITION: June 2003

COMPLETION DATE: 2008 (projected)

CLIENT: Toronto International Film Festival Group

PROGRAM: 42-storey mixed-use development including 5-storey base comprising 150,000 sq. ft. of flexible, multi-use space, including three cinemas and two flexible screening spaces for total of 1,300 cinema seats; 37 floor residential condominium tower

COMPETITION TEAM: Bruce Kuwabara, Shirley Blumberg, Luigi LaRocca, Bruno Weber, Brent Wagler, Tyler Sharp, Esther Cheung

KPMB ARCHITECTS: Bruce Kuwabara (design partner); Shirley Blumberg (partner-in-charge); Luigi LaRocca (associate-in-charge); Bruno Weber, Brent Wagler, Tyler Sharp (project architects)

ARCHITECT OF RECORD: Kirkor Architects and Planner

ENGINEERS: Jablonsky, Ast and Partners (structural), LKM (mechanical and electrical)

DIGITAL RENDERINGS: Norm Li

MODEL: JS Models, Jack Szymoniak

MODEL PHOTO: Ben Rahn / A Frame, Toronto

Gardiner Museum of Ceramic Art

LOCATION: Queen's Park Crescent, Toronto, Ontario

COMPLETION DATE: 2005

CLIENT: The George R. Gardiner Museum of Ceramic Art

PROGRAM: 33,886 sq. ft. renovation and addition of gallery space

CONTRACT VALUE: $10 million

KPMB ARCHITECTS: Bruce Kuwabara (design partner); Shirley Blumberg (partner-in-charge); Paulo Rocha (project architect); Shane O'Neill, Javier Uribe, Kevin Bridgman, Tyler Sharp, Ramon Janer, Bill Colaco (project team)

ENGINEERS: Halsall Associates Ltd. (structural), Crossey Engineering Ltd. (mechanical and electrical),

CONSULTANTS: Leber-Rubes Inc. (fire and life safety), Vermeulens Cost Consultants (cost), Soberman Engineering (elevator), Suzanne Powadiuk (lighting)

Le Quartier Concordia, Concordia University

LOCATION: Two parcels of land bounded by Ste-Catherine Street, Boulevard de Maisonneuve, Pierce and Mackay, Montréal, Québec

COMPETITION DATE: November 2000

COMPLETION DATE: Engineering/Computer Science and Visual Arts: Spring 2005; John Molson School of Business: Spring 2006

CLIENT: Concordia University

PROGRAM: John Molson School of Business (JMSB): 350,000 sq. ft.; Engineering/Computer Science (ECS): 500,000 sq. ft.; Visual Arts (VA): 150,000 sq. ft.

CONTRACT VALUE: $195 million (estimated)

COMPETITION TEAM: Bruce Kuwabara, Paulo Rocha, Marianne McKenna, Andrew Dyke, Julie Dionne, Catherine Venart

JOINT VENTURE ARCHITECTS: Architects Kuwabara Payne McKenna Blumberg Architects / Fichten Soiferman et Associés Architectes, architects in joint venture

KPMB ARCHITECTS: John Molson School of Business: Bruce Kuwabara (design partner); Marianne McKenna (partner-in-charge); Andrew Dyke (associate); John Peterson, Glen MacMullin, Robert Kastelic (project architects); Lucy Timbers, Eric Ho, Paolo Zasso, André Préfontaine, Omar Gandhi, Jill Osiowy (project team). Engineering/Computer Science and Visual Arts: Bruce Kuwabara (design partner); Marianne McKenna (partner-in-charge); Andrew Dyke (associate); Anne Marie Fleming, Glenn MacMullin, Bill Colaco, Lucy Timbers, Rita Kiriakis, Eric Ho, Chris Wegner, Meika McCunn, Paolo Zasso, André Préfontaine, Dan Nawrocki, Deborah Wang (project team)

FSA ARCHITECTES: Jacob Fichten (partner-in-charge), Gerald Soiferman (partner, administration); Engineering: Andrij Serbyn (production and site), Julie Dionne, Eugeno Laborde, Bertrand Marais, Michael Hall, Bernard Jacques, André Tremblay, Nicholas-Mallik Paquin, Ngae-Chi Wong, Benoit Picard, Sandrine Zambo, Xin Wu; Visual Arts: Andrij Serbyn (production and site), Julie Dionne, Victor Gazon, Bertrand Marais, Michael Hall; John Molson: Artur Kobylanski, Demitri Koubatis, Martine Lacombe, Eric Jofriet, Leila Palumbo

ENGINEERS: John Molson School of Business: Nicolet Chartrand Knoll Limitée (structural), Groupe HBA Experts-Conseils Senc. (mechanical and electrical). Engineering/Computer Science and Visual Arts: Nicolet Chartrand Knoll Limitée (structural), Pageau Morel et Associés, Dupras Ledux Ingenieurs, Keen Engineering (mechanical, electrical and sustainability)

CONSULTANTS: John Molson School of Business: Leber Rubes Inc. and Curran McCabe Ravindran, Technorm Inc. (code and safety); Exim (vertical transportation); Trizart Alliance (audio/visual); Doucet et Associés (IT/Security); Brook Van Dalen Associates (building envelope). Engineering/Computer Science and Visual Arts: Curran McCabe Ravindran Ross Inc. (cost), Leber Rubes Inc./Technorm Inc.

PROJECT MANAGER: Gespro S.S.T. Inc.

GENERAL CONTRACTOR: Pomerleau (for Engineering and Computer Science/Visual Arts)

MODEL RENDERINGS: Q-Studio, Toronto

PHOTOGRAPHY: Michel Brunelle, Montréal

Royal Conservatory of Music Performance and Learning Centre

LOCATION: 273 Bloor Street West, Toronto

COMPLETION DATE: 2006

CLIENT: Royal Conservatory of Music

PROGRAM: A new 124,000 sq. ft. performance and learning centre, including 1,100-seat concert hall, 23,000 sq. ft. rehearsal room and 55 practice studios; renovation of 54,000 sq. ft. heritage building into integrated building complex

KPMB ARCHITECTS: Marianne McKenna (partner-in-charge); Robert Sims (associate); Dan Benson, Meika McCunn, Chris Wegner, Bill Colaco, George Friedman, Erik Jenson, Mark Simpson, Krista Clark, Lexi Kolt Wagner, Clare Radford, Jill Osiowy, Deborah Wang, Norm Li, Rita Kiriakis, Dave Smythe, Scott Pomeroy (project team)

LANDSCAPE ARCHITECT: Janet Rosenberg & Associates Inc.

ENGINEERS: Yolles Partnership (structural), Merber Corporation (mechanical), Crossey Engineering Ltd. (electrical), Brook Van Dalen Associates (building envelope), A.M. Candaras Associates Inc. (civil)

CONSULTANTS: Aercoustics Engineering Ltd. (acoustics), Sound Space Design — Bob Essert (acoustics), Anne Minors Performance Consultants (theatre), Office for Visual Interaction Inc-OVI (lighting), Soberman Engineering (vertical transportation), Goldsmith Borgal & Company Ltd. (heritage), Curran McCabe Ravindran Ross (cost), Leber/Rubes Inc. (code), LEA Consulting Ltd. (traffic), Brook Van Dalen Associates (building envelope)

PROJECT MANAGER: Paul Hatton (PHA Project Management)

MODELS: Jack Symoniak (JS Models), Erik Jensen, Mark Simpson

COMPUTER RENDERINGS: Q Studio, Toronto; Norm Li

PHOTOGRAPHS: Robert Burley/Design Archive (model shots)

Vaughan Civic Centre

LOCATION: Vaughan, Ontario

COMPETITION: 2004

COMPLETION DATE: 2010 (projected)

CLIENT: City of Vaughan

PROGRAM: 325,000 sq. ft., including city hall, civic tower, council chambers and civic administration offices; reference library; Hydro Vaughan Distribution Inc.; Chamber of Commerce; landscape elements include a Civic Square, reflecting pool/skating rink, public gardens and naturalized park

CONTRACT VALUE: $76 million (initial budget)

COMPETITION TEAM: Bruce Kuwabara (partner); Luigi LaRocca (senior associate); Kevin Bridgman (project architect); Tyler Sharp, Andrea Macaroun, Javier Uribe, Norm Li (project team)

ENGINEERS: Yolles Partnership Inc. (Structural Engineers), Keen Engineering (Mechanical Engineers & Sustainability Consultants), Mulvey & Banani International Inc. (Electrical Engineers), Philips Farvaag Smallenberg (Landscape Architects), LEA Consulting Ltd. (Traffic & Municipal Consultants), DST Consulting Engineers (LEED Consultants)

Young Centre for the Performing Arts

LOCATION: Gooderham & Worts Distillery, Tanks 9 and 10, Toronto, Ontario

COMPLETION DATE: 2005

CLIENT: George Brown College and Soulpepper Theatre Company

PROGRAMS: 400-seat flexible theatre, 200-seat flexible format dance theatre, three 100-seat studio theatres, rehearsal/teaching studios, performance support spaces, workshop facilities, lobby and ticketing facilities, and administrative offices for both organizations

CONTRACT VALUE: tbd

KPMB ARCHITECTS: Thomas Payne (partner-in-charge); Chris Couse (senior associate); Mark Jaffar, Ann Lok (project architects)

ENGINEERS: Read Jones Christoffersen Limited (structural), Crossey Engineering (mechanical and electrical)

CONSULTANTS: Theatre Projects Consultants (theatre), Aercoustics Engineering (acoustical)

PROJECT MANAGER: PHA Project Management Inc.

SITE PHOTOS: Robert Hill, Toronto

JOINT VENTURES AND ASSOCIATIONS

Canadian Embassy, Berlin, Germany
Kuwabara Payne McKenna Blumberg Architects /
Gagnon Letellier Cyr, Architectes, and Smith Carter
Architects + Engineers Inc., joint venture
architects

Cardinal Ambrozic Houses of Providence
Montgomery and Sisam Architects, Kuwabara Payne
McKenna Blumberg Architects, joint venture
architects

Centennial HP Science and Technology Centre, Centennial College
Kuwabara Payne McKenna Blumberg Architects /
Stone McQuire Vogt Architects, associated
architects

Chinese Cultural Centre
Kuwabara Payne McKenna Blumberg Architects in
joint venture with Patrick T. Y. Chan Architect
KPMB ARCHITECTS: Bruce Kuwabara (partner-in-charge);
Andrew Dyke (project architect); John Allen, Don
Collins, Gerry Lang (project team)
PATRICK T. Y. CHAN ARCHITECT: Patrick Chan (partner-in-
charge); Danny Teh (project architect); Ky Maruyama

Goodman Theater
Kuwabara Payne McKenna Blumberg Architects,
DLK Architecture Inc., McClier Corporation,
associated architects for The Goodman Theater

Genomics and Proteomics Research Building, McGill University
Kuwabara Payne McKenna Blumberg Architects /
Fichten Soiferman et Associés, Architectes,
architects in joint venture

Le Quartier Concordia, Concordia University
Kuwabara Payne McKenna Blumberg Architects /
Fichten Soiferman et Associés, Architectes,
architects in joint venture

Maple Leaf Lounge, Pearson International Airport
Kuwabara Payne McKenna Blumberg Architects in
association with II by IV Design Associates Inc.,
NORR Limited, Architects and Engineers
(Architects of Record)
COMPETITION TEAM: Bruce Kuwabara (partner-in-
charge); Kevin Thomas, Carolyn Lee, Maryam
Nourmansouri.

KPMB ARCHITECTS: Bruce Kuwabara (partner-in-charge);
Luigi Larocca (senior associate); Olga Pushkar,
Steven Casey (project architects); Dan Nawrocki,
Carolyn Lee (project team)
II X V DESIGN ASSOCIATES INC.: Dan Menchions, Keith
Rushbrook (partners-in-charge)

The National Ballet School, Toronto
Kuwabara Payne McKenna Blumberg Architects,
Goldsmith Borgal and Company Ltd., architects in
joint venture
KPMB ARCHITECTS: Bruce Kuwabara (design partner);
Shirley Blumberg (partner-in-charge); Mitchell
Hall (associate/project architect); Olga Pushkar,
Myriam Tawadros, Ramon Janer, Jeff Strauss,
Norm Li, Jimmy Sun, Jill Osiowy, Maryam
Nourmansouri, Henry Burstyn, Catherine Venart,
Riki Nishimura, Samer Hoot (project team)
GOLDSMITH BORGAL AND COMPANY: Phil Goldsmith
(partner-in-charge); Paul Gagné, Allan Killin

Canadian Museum of Nature, Ottawa
Padolsky, Kuwabara, Gagnon (PKG), architects in joint
venture
ASSOCIATE ARCHITECT: Barry Padolsky Associates Inc.,
Architect
ASSOCIATE ARCHITECT: Kuwabara Payne McKenna
Blumberg Architects
ASSOCIATE ARCHITECT: Gagnon Letellier Cyr, Architectes
BARRY PADOLSKY ARCHITECTS: Barry Padolsky (PKG project
manager); Louise McGugan (project architect); Paul
Dolan (PKG project coordinator); Rebecca Aiken,
Peter Elliott, Eric Fruhauf, Tony Hamilton, Elizabeth
Saikali, Jason Sheldrick, Grant Stewart (project team)
KPMB ARCHITECTS: Bruce Kuwabara (partner-in-charge,
design); Brent Wagler (project architect); Bruno
Weber, Jose Emila, Andrew Gunn, Tom Knezic,
Esther Cheung, Yekta Pakdaman-Hamedani, Tyler
Sharp (project team)
GAGNON LETELLIER CYR, ARCHITECTES: Marc Letellier,
Michel Gagnon (partners-in-charge); Suzanne
Castonguay, Jean-Nicolas Faguy, Jean-Sébastien
Laberge, Vincent Lavoie, Pierre Michaud, Nicolas
Mallik Paquin, Réal St.-Pierre (project team)

Woodsworth College, University of Toronto
Barton Myers Architect Inc. / Kuwabara Payne McKenna
Blumberg Architects, associated architects

Selected Bibliography

General articles on KPMB

Bachmann, Wolfgang. "Architektur in Kanada." *Baumeister* (Germany) Vol. 4 (April 1995): 17, 19, 102

Blore, Shawn. "Construction Crew: Building a New Architectural Model with KPMB." *Enroute* (March 2001): 51–60

Fisher, Thomas and Steven Fong. "Emerging Talent: Kuwabara Payne McKenna Blumberg." *Progressive Architecture* (October 1992): 96–103

Kuwabara Payne McKenna Blumberg, a monograph in the *Contemporary World Architects* series. USA: Rockport Publishers Inc., 1998. (foreword by George Baird; introduction by Detlef Mertins)

"Kuwabara Payne McKenna Blumberg Architects: the first three projects." *Contract Magazine* (April/May 1991): 32–34

Ammirati Puris Lintas, New York

"Agencia de Publicidad APL en Manhattan." *Diseño Interior* (Spain) No. 71 (February 1998): 84–89 [Spanish text]

Bierman, Lindsay. "Light on White." *Interior Design* (January 1997): 108–115

Cerver, F.A. *Extraordinary Offices*. USA: Watson Guptill, 1998. 58–63

Kapusta, Beth. "Interior Architecture: White on White." *Canadian Architect* (October 1996): 26–29

Canadian Embassy, Berlin, Germany

Collyer, Stanley. "A Building Block for Berlin." *Competitions Magazine* (Spring 1999): 34–37

"Friendly and Inviting: Canada's New Embassy at Leipziger Platz in Berlin." *Deutschland* (Germany) (August/September 1999): 33

"Loeffler, Jane. "Post Terror Diplomacy." *Interiors* (April 2000): 48–51

Weder, Adele. "A Berlin Chronicle." *Canadian Architect* (June 1999): 20–21

"Nordwest-Passage: Leipziger Platz 17," in L. Back and L. Demps, *Der Leipziger Platz: Gestern und morgen*. Berlin: Verlaghaus Braun, 2002. 118–119 [German text]

Cardinal Ambrozic Houses of Providence, Scarborough, Ontario

Levitt, Andrew. "Houses to Call Home." *Canadian Architect* (November 2000): 26–29

Young, Pamela. "Humanizing Long Term Care." *Insite* (March 1996): 33–35

Young, Pamela. "The Age Factor." *Azure* (September/October 2000): 90–95

Chinese Cultural Centre, Scarborough, Ontario

"Chinese Cultural Centre." *Competitions Magazine* (Winter 1998/99): 40–41

Fong, Steven. "The Culture of Building/The Building of Culture." *Canadian Architect* (February 1999): 26–29

Social Spaces of the World Vol. 1. Melbourne: Images Publishing Group, 2000. 10–11, 215

Design Exchange, Toronto

Betsky, Aaron. "Design for Living or Selling?" *Metropolis* (May 1995): 120–123

Hoyt, Charles K. "Challenging Exchange." *Architectural Record* (September 1995): 86–89

Linton, Harold. *Color in Architecture: Design Methods for Buildings, Interiors and Urban Spaces*. New York: McGraw Hill, 1999. 24–30

Morawetz, Tim. "Shirley Blumberg: Building an Architecture of Inclusion." *Exchange: A Review of Design and Innovation* Vol. 3, No. 1 (February 1994) [interview]

Richards, Larry Wayne. "Designing Bridges: The Spirit and Space of KPMB," in *Designing the Exchange: Essays Commemorating the Opening of the Design Exchange*. Toronto: 1994. 17–29

Rodger, Nelda. "Built for Endurance." *Azure* (November/December 1994): 23–25

van der Neut, Rund. "Toronto Design Exchange." *Objekt Magazine* (Netherlands) No. 18 (Spring 2001): 100–103

Downsview Park Competition, Toronto

Mertins, Detlef, "Downsview Park: International Design Competition." *Quaderni PPC* (Italy) No. 2 (March 2003): 84–87

Czerniak, Julia. *Downsview Park, Toronto*. München: Prestel Verlag, 2002. 66–73

Kapelos, George. "Less is More." *Competitions Magazine* Vol. 10, No. 3 (Fall 2000): 28–43

Polo, Marco. "Environment as Process." *Canadian Architect* (October 2000): 14–19

"Sui parchi tematici/ On Theme Parks." *LOTUS International* (Italy) No. 109 (1999): 36–39

Genomics and Proteomics Research Building, McGill University, Montréal

Phillips, Rhys. "Building Code: New Research Facility." *Building Magazine* (December/January 2004): 32–34.

Strickland, Tom. "Façade Fabric 2: The Genome Centre, McGill University." *ON/SITE Review* No. 8 (Spring 2003): 23–25.

Goodman Theater, Chicago

Warson, Albert. "Two Toronto Firms Win Prized U.S. Commissions: How'd They Do That?" *Architectural Record* (June 2000): 45

Grand Valley Institution for Women, Kitchener, Ontario

Justice Facilities Review 1997–1998. Washington, D.C.: The American Institute of Architects, Committee on Architecture for Justice. 2–5

Kapusta, Beth. "Grand Valley Institution for Women." *Architectural Record* (December 1998): 72–75

Macdonald, Marie-Paule. "Correctional Facilities — Instituting Domesticity." *Canadian Architect* (November 1998): 34–39

MacInnes, Katherine. "Grand Valley Institution for Women, Ontario, Canada." *World Architecture* (London) No. 73 (February 1999): 106–107

Weder, Adele. "A Women's Place." *Azure* (March/April 1999): 50–54

Hilton Toronto, Toronto

Ota, John. "Executive Romantic." *Canadian Architect* (September 2002): 32–36

Renzi, Jan. "Lobbying for Change." *Interior Design*, First Annual Hospitality Awards (January 2001): 232–235

Jackson-Triggs Niagara Estate Winery, Niagara-on-the-Lake, Ontario

"Business Week/Architectural Awards Finalist: Architecture Toasts the Success of Wine." *Architectural Record* (November 2003): 106

Kim, Sheila. "Clearly Canadian." *Interior Design* (January 2002): 194, 214–216 [Hospitality Awards]

Polo, Marco. "In Vino Veritas." *Canadian Architect* (October 2001): 19–23

Young, Pamela. "A Cellar Attraction." *Azure* (November/ December 2001): 56–60

James Stewart Centre for Mathematics, McMaster University, Hamilton, Ontario

Kapusta, Beth. "Creative Edition." *Azure* (March/April 2004): 90–93

Japanese Canadian Cultural Centre, Toronto

Ota, John. "Turning Eastward." *Azure* (November/ December 1999): 46–47

Joseph S. Stauffer Library, Queen's University, Kingston, Ontario

Ammaturo, Laura. "La biblioteca della Queen's University a Kingston." *l'ARCA* (Italy) No. 52 (September 1991): 97–98

Benson, Robert A. "Tradition in Transition." *Canadian Architect* (August 1995): 20–25

Freedman, Adele. "Contempo-Gothic for Canadian Library." *Progressive Architecture* (April 1991): 21

Freedman, Adele. "Gothic Humanism." *Architecture* (February 1995): 86–93

"Joseph S. Stauffer Library." *Architecture and Urbanism* (Japan) No. 305 (February 1996): 40–47

"Joseph Stauffer Library, Kingston." *World Architecture* (China) No. 136 (October 2001): 32–36

King James Place, Toronto

Governor General's Awards for Architecture 1992. Ottawa: The Royal Architectural Institute of Canada, 1992. 96–101

Grassi, Marco. "King James Place a Toronto." *Costruire in Laterizio* (Italy) No. 65 (September/October 1998): 322–327

Kitchener City Hall, Kitchener, Ontario

Bachmann, Wolfgang. "Architektur in Kanada." *Baumeister* (Germany) Vol. 4 (April 1995): 17, 102

Bierman, M. Lindsay. "Canadian Civitas." *Architecture* Vol. 9 (September 1994): 88–93

Bleznick, Susan R. "Kitchener's New Municipal Centre." *Architectural Record* (January 1990): 30–31

Carter, Brian. "Civic Sensibility." *The Architectural Review* No. 1172 (October 1994): 58–61

Collyer, Stanley. "Interview: Bruce Kuwabara." *Competitions Magazine* (Winter 1998–99): 34–37

Frampton, Kenneth. "Intimate Monumentality." *Canadian Architect* Vol. 39, No. 7 (July 1994): 17–25

"Kitchener City Hall Competition: Winner." *Canadian Architect* (November 1989): 34–38

Mertins, Detlef, and Virginia Wright, editors. *Competing Visions: The Kitchener City Hall Competition.* Toronto: The Melting Press, 1990

Owen, Graham, ed. "Kitchener City Hall & Civic Square." *The Governor General's Awards for Architecture, 1994.* Ottawa: The Royal Architectural Institute of Canada (1994): 76–83

Terzi, Giovanni. "Il municipio di Kitchener." *l'ARCA* (Italy) No. 80 (March 1994): 58–65

Le Quartier Concordia, Concordia University, Montréal

"Concordia selects architects for downtown complex." *Canadian Interiors* (January/February 2001): 6

"Concours d'architecture Université Concordia," *ARQ* Vol. 117 (November 2001): 16–21, 24.

Marc Laurent, Toronto

"Bruce Kuwabara, Thomas Payne, Negozio di Abbigliamento, Toronto." *Domus* (Italy) (July/August 1990): 6–8

Kitagawa, Machiko. "Marc Laurent." *Pronto* (Japan) Vol. 3, No. 4 (1991): 10–11

"Kuwabara Payne McKenna Blumberg Architects: The First Three Projects." *Contract Magazine* (April/May 1991): 40–42

Cawker, Ruth. "Marc Laurent Store." *Toronto: Le Nouveau Nouveau Monde* (March 1987): 36–37 [exhibition guide, Paris].

"Marc Laurent Store Expansion." *Canadian Architect* (September 1989): 28–30

Truppin, Andrea. "Canadian Design." *Interiors* (March 1989): 112–113

Reisman-Jenkinson Residence, Richmond Hill, Ontario

Fisher, Thomas. "Three Properties." *Canadian Architect* (January 1995): 14–17

Owen, Graham, ed. "Reisman-Jenkinson Residence and Studio," in *The Governor General's Awards for Architecture, 1994.* Ottawa: The Royal Architectural Institute of Canada, 1994. 174–181

Pignatti, Lorenzo. "Bruce Kuwabara, Evan Webber: Residence and Studio, Richmond Hill, Ontario." *Domus* (Italy) No. 764 (October 1994): 43–47

Richmond City Hall, Richmond, British Columbia

Luymes, Don. "Reinventing Suburban Identity." *Landscape Architecture* (July 2002): 60–65

Polo, Marco. "Brilliant Green." *Canadian Architect* (January 2001): 20–25

"Richmond City Hall." *Competitions Magazine* (Winter 1998/99): 38–39

"Richmond City Hall." *Governor General's Medals in Architecture.* Ottawa: Royal Architectural Institute of Canada, 2002. 36–43

Roy Thomson Hall Enhancement, Toronto

Kirk, Fion. "Canadian Glory." *Stage Directions* (April 2003): 32–35

Rose, Allison. "Seen and Heard: Roy Thomson Hall." *Canadian Architect* (November 2002): 20–23

Ravine House, Toronto

"Award: Residential Category A — Single Family Residence — Sheff House." *OAA Perspectives*, Vol 11, No. 2 (Summer 2003): 12–13.

Browne, Kelvin. "Dream Houses." *Toronto Life* (October 2003): 92–93

"Kalifornien am Lake Ontario," in *Häuser* (Germany) (January 2004): 44–51 (German text), English translation page iv. Photographs by Jürgen Franke

Star Alliance Lounge, Zurich International Airport, Switzerland

"Frequent flyers' reward." *Canadian Interiors* (July/August 2002): 50 [Best of Canada Award]

"Garten im Flughafen." *Hochparterre* (Switzerland) (November 2001): 67

Lasker, David. "KPMB Rethinks the Airline Lounge." *Canadian Interiors* (March/April 2002): 39–42

"Terminal Well-Being." *Wallpaper* (October 2001): 364

Tudhope Studios, Toronto

Stein, Karen. "A Plane Solution." *Architectural Record* (July 1990): 60–63

Woodsworth College, University of Toronto, Toronto

Fong, Stephen. "Representing the Academic Village." *Progressive Architecture* (October 1992): 100–103

Owen, Graham. "Woodsworth College: Generosity of Mind and Materials." *International Contract* Vol. 1, No. 7 (August/September 1992): 51–54

Richardson, Douglas. *The New Woodsworth College.* Photographs by Steven Evans. Toronto: Woodsworth College, University of Toronto, 1994

Sayah, Amber. "College in Toronto; Architekten: KPMB mit Barton Myers." *Baumeister* (Germany) Vol. 4 (April 1995): 25–29

The Governor General's Awards for Architecture 1992. Ottawa: The Royal Architectural Institute of Canada, 1992. 52–57

"University Challenge." *Architectural Review* (May 1993): 57–61

Partner Biographies

Kuwabara Payne McKenna Blumberg Architects (KPMB)
KPMB was founded in 1987 by Bruce Kuwabara, Thomas Payne, Marianne McKenna, and Shirley Blumberg. The firm established its reputation in the first five years of practice by winning the design competitions for Kitchener City Hall and the Joseph S. Stauffer Library at Queen's University in Kingston. Since then the firm has expanded its practice with projects in the United States and Europe, including the Canadian Embassy in Berlin, Germany. KPMB's contribution to the quality of contemporary Canadian architecture is recognized by nine Governor General's Awards for Architecture, Canada's highest architectural honour.

BRUCE KUWABARA, born in Hamilton, Ontario, in 1949. Completed architectural studies at the University of Toronto. Worked for George Baird before joining Barton Myers Associates, Toronto, in 1975. Visiting lecturer at the University of California at Los Angeles from 1979–81. Adjunct associate professor at the University of Toronto since 1987. Visiting adjunct professor at Harvard University in 1990–91. Co-chair at the Faculty of Architecture, Landscape and Design at the University of Toronto since 1998. He has been a visiting critic and guest lecturer at various Canadian and American universities.

THOMAS PAYNE, born in Chatham, Ontario, in 1949. Architectural studies at Princeton University, l'École des Beaux-Arts, Paris, and Yale University, where he completed his Master's degree in 1974. Worked for John Andrews International Architects, Sydney, before moving to Toronto in 1979. There he worked first for George Baird before joining Barton Myers Associates for eight years. He was a studio critic at Harvard University's Graduate School of Design in 1981 and a thesis advisor at the University of Toronto from 1986–89.

MARIANNE MCKENNA, born in Montréal, Québec, in 1950. Studied at Swarthmore College Philadelphia, B.A. 1972, and Yale University, where she completed her Master of Architecture degree in 1976. Worked for Bobrow & Fieldman, Montréal, from 1976–78, and for Denys Lasdun, Redhouse & Softley, London, from 1978–79. Joined Barton Myers Associates in Toronto in 1980 until 1987. Has served various academic and design critic functions at McGill University (1979–80), the Université de Montréal (1991–93, 1994), the University of Toronto (1993–95), Yale University (1994–95) and again at McGill since 1997.

SHIRLEY BLUMBERG, born in Cape Town, South Africa, in 1952. Architectural studies at the University of Cape Town and the University of Toronto where she graduated in 1976 with a Bachelor of Architecture (Honours). Joined Barton Myers Associates, Toronto, in 1977. Academically she has been a lecturer and visiting critic at several universities in Canada and the United States. In particular, she has served at the University of Toronto as adjunct assistant professor (1987, 1989–90) and as thesis tutor from 1997–98 and in 2001. In 1994, she became the First Woman Appointee to the Hyde Chair for Excellence in Architecture at the University of Nebraska-Lincoln.

Competitions

1987   Ottawa City Hall, Ottawa
1989   Kitchener City Hall, open national competition, Kitchener, Ontario (winner)
        Queen's University, Joseph S. Stauffer Library, invited competition, Kingston, Ontario (winner)
1990   Markborough/Trizec, Toronto
1991   Vancouver Library Square, Vancouver
        Chinese Cultural Centre, Scarborough, Ontario (winner)
        University of Waterloo Student Centre, Waterloo, Ontario
        Oakville Parks, Oakville, Ontario (winner)
1994   Tip Top Tailors, Toronto
1995   KOMA (Korean Museum of Art), open international competition, Los Angeles (honorable mention)
1996   University of Waterloo Environmental Sciences Building, Waterloo, Ontario
        Centre for International Studies, University of Toronto, Toronto (winner)
1998   Canadian Embassy, Berlin, Germany (winner)
        York University Gates, North York, Ontario
        Hamilton Art Gallery, Hamilton, Ontario (winner)
1999   IMCA Competition, Calgary, Alberta
        Information Technology Centre, University of Toronto, Toronto
        Denver Civic Centre, Denver, Colorado
        Downsview Park Competition, Toronto

2000   Concordia University Integrated Academic Complex, Montréal (winner)
        Star Alliance Lounge, Zurich International Airport, Switzerland (winner)
2001   Centre for Addiction and Mental Health Complex, Toronto (winner)
        Canada Life Federal Courts Building, Toronto (winner)
2002   University of Toronto Pharmacy Building, Toronto
2003   Bank Street Building, Parliament Hill, Ottawa
        Festival Centre and Tower, Toronto International Film Festival, Toronto (winner)
2004   Vaughan City Hall, Vaughan, Ontario (winner)

Acknowledgements

We thank our clients for their vision and for creating the opportunities that have allowed us to make the architecture which this book celebrates.

We would like to thank all the individuals who have contributed to our practice over the last seventeen years, and to acknowledge their talent, dedication and tenacity. All have made a significant contribution to our work. In particular, we thank our senior associates Chris Couse and Luigi LaRocca, who have been with us from the beginning, giving us stability, pragmatic vision, and without whose unwavering loyalty, professionalism, and architectural expertise we could not make the work that we do.

Our deep appreciation to our associates who have contributed to the quality of the work of the studio. In particular, we acknowledge their work on the projects that appear in this book. Goran Milosevic whose unrelenting dedication to the Raether Library at Trinity College over the last five years has ensured such high quality results. Mitchell Hall for his strong design talent, passionate commitment, and brilliant execution of the Jackson-Triggs Winery and the Genomics and Proteomics Research Building at McGill University. Andrew Dyke who was crucial to the design and development of the Canadian Embassy in Berlin and Le Quartier Concordia at Concordia University in Montréal. David Jesson for his spirited creativity and attention to detail on the Hilton Toronto and Roy Thomson Hall projects. Bob Sims for his thoughtful contributions and unwavering dedication to St. Andrew's College and the Royal Conservatory of Music Performance and Learning Centre. Judy Taylor for her superb professionalism and effective leadership on the Richmond City Hall project. John Allen who has ensured the flawless execution of our most highly complex projects, from Kitchener City Hall, the Grand Valley Institution and onward.

We also thank all those who keep us challenged and growing, and who have provided critical contributions to the design development of our best work in the last five years: Kevin Bridgman, Mark Jaffar, Rob Kastelic, Glenn MacMullin, John Peterson, David Poloway, Olga Pushkar, Paulo Rocha, Brent Wagler, Bruno Weber and Matthew Wilson.

Our thanks to Daphne Harris, who has kept us on the straight and narrow fiscally. Robert Hill for his invaluable research and photography skills, his encyclopædic knowledge of Canadian architecture, and his unending energy without which the studio would not function as efficiently as it does. And, our loyal administrative staff, for their ongoing patience and support.

We would also like to give special mention to our many collaborators: our superb joint venture partners, our longstanding and talented engineers and consultants, and the skilled contractors who have so effectively realized our projects, and who are all noted in the project credits of this book.

In the making of this book, we would also like to acknowledge Oscar Riera Ojeda who was the catalyst for this publication and introduced us to Birkhäuser. Our thanks to Amanda Sebris without whose single-minded enthusiasm, persistence and rigour this book would not have happened. Special thanks to Kevin Bridgman for offering his critical eye and moral support. We also thank Ante Liu who introduced us to Jeanna South and Sylvain Bombardier, who prepared the drawings for this publication with professionalism, grace and patience. Our particular gratitude to Kathleen Oginski for capturing so aptly the spirit of our work in her design, and to Ria Stein and Michael Wachholz of Birkhäuser for their editorial wisdom, support and enthusiasm.

Our sincere thanks to Phyllis Lambert, Detlef Mertins, Bruce Mau and Rodolphe el-Khoury for their generous and insightful contributions to this monograph.

Finally, with deepest gratitude and appreciation to our greatest supporters—our families and partners who have shown incredible patience and unwavering faith through the years.

Staff 1987-2004

Safdar Abidi
John Agnidis
John Allen
Pamela Allen
Fred Allin
Andrew Alzner
Kyle Anderson
Michael Awad

Taymore Balboa
Anna Baraness
Neil Bauman
Chris Beamer
Daniel Benson
Rob Beraldo
Mark Berest
Adrian Blackwell
Andrew Blackwood
Kevin Bridgman
Jillian Brown
Kelly Buffey
Henry Burstyn
Andrew Butler

Jill Calvert
Franziska Cape
Byron Carter
Allison Carr
Steven Casey
Vince Catalli
Clementine Chang
Rosa Chang
Natalie Cheng
Esther Cheung
Donald Chong
Kim Chong
Kelly Chow
Larry Chow
Nicholas Choy
Chester Chu
Mark Cichy
Andrea Clark
Krista Clark
Kyra Clarkson
Bill Colaco
Donald Collins
John Cook
Christopher Couse
Karen Cvornyek
John Czechowski
Lisa d'Abbondanza

Andre D'Elia
Deni DiFilippo
Walter Daschko
Matthew Dawson
Elaine Didyk
Virginia Dos Reis
Heather Dubbeldam
Gwen Duggan
Andrew Dyke

Amin Ebrahim
Jose Emila
Michael Epp
Janine Ewart

Robert Faber
Deborah Fabricius
Shaun Fernandes
Graham Ferrier
Mary Jane Finlayson
Anne-Marie Fleming
George Friedman

Dominic Gagnon
Rick Galezowski
Omar Gandhi
Joan Gardner
Walter Gaudet
Shauna Gilles-Smith
Rob Gilvesey
Kelvin Goddard
Valerie Gow
Brian Graham
Meg Graham
Bill Greaves
Victoria Gregory
Chanzy Gu
Greg Guerra
Don Gulay
Andrew Gunn

Mitchell Hall
Siamak Hariri
Daphne Harris
Simon Haus
Courtney Henry
Robert G. Hill
Monica Hlozanek
Wai Cheong (Eric) Ho
Tina Hollinshead
Samer Hoot
Rick Hopkins
Beverly Horii

Desmond Hui
Grant Hutchinson

Michael Isaac
Ian Izukawa

Mark Jaffar
Prish Jain
Ramon Janer
Erik Jensen
David Jesson
Forde Johnson
Andrew Jones

Wendy Kaiser
Rob Kastelic
Joo-Hwan (Terry) Kim
Jason King
Rita Kiriakis
Tomislav Knezic
Tom Koehler
Lexi Kolt-Wagner
Andrea Kordos
Tom Kraljevic
Michael Krus
Jennifer Kuwabara
Dace Kuze
Nelson Kwong

Alex Lam
Gerry Lang
Luigi LaRocca
Jeff Latto
Annette Lee
Brian Lee
Carolyn Lee
Jyh-Ling Lee
Kelly Lem
Aaron Letki
Alan Leung
Christine Levine
Norm Li
Jason Lin
Diana Yun Liu
Leslie Livingston
Mary Lou Lobsinger
Anne Lok
Ken Lum
Chris Lyle

Andrea Macaroun
Andrea MacElwee
James MacGillivray
Lara MacInnis
Glenn MacMullin
Todd Macyk
Marco Magarelli
Leah Maguire
Brian Main
Karen Mak
Glen Man
Drew Mandel
Phil Marjeram
Katya Marshall
Kevin Mast
Andrew Masuda
Anita Matusevics
Michelle Mearns
Meika McCunn
Paul McDonnell
Shannon McGaw
Heidi McKenzie
Peter McMillan
Dan McNeil
Gianni Meogrossi
Goran Milosevic
Devorah Miller
Neil Morfitt
Joe Moro
Joanne Myers

Dan Nawrocki
Joseph Neuwirth
Riki Nishimura
Maryam Nourmansouri

Yusuke Obuchi
Roy Oei
Meelena Oleksiuk-Baker
Shane O'Neill
Sean O'Reilly
Quinlan Osborne
Jill Osiowy
Graham Owen

Yekta Pakdaman-
Hamedani
Lheila Palumbo
Miyako Panalaks
Katherine Pankratz
Glenn Parker
Juliette Patterson
Karen Pawluk

Jason Pearson
Dmytriy Pereklita
John Peterson
Karen Petrachenko
Sheryl Phillips
Mike Poitras
David Poloway
Scott Pomeroy
David Pontarini
Frank Portelli
Suzanne Powadiuk
Andre Provencher
Anthony Provenzano
Olga Pushkar

Andres Quinlan

Shadi Rahbaran
Clare Radford
Johanna Radix
Ron Renters
Corry Ricci
Howard Rideout
Steven Robinson
Paulo Rocha
Jerry Rubin

Shabbar Sagarwala
Amanda Sebris
Thom Seto
Tyler Sharp
Leslie Shimotakahara
John Shnier
Birgit Siber
Mark A. Simone
Marc Simmons
Mark Simpson
Bob Sims
Andrew Sinclair
Danny Sinopoli
Lola Skytt
Cal Smith
David Smythe
Jeanna South
Carolyn Steele
Olesia Stefurak
Chris Stevens
Jeff Strauss
Dawn Stremler
Tom Strickland
Jimmy Sun
Howard Sutcliffe
Talbot Sweetapple

Myriam Tawadros
Sherene Tay
Judy Taylor
Michael Taylor
Simon Taylor
Kevin Thomas
Lucy Timbers
Jennifer Ting
Janet Town
Kathleen Triggs
Jennifer Turner
Sylvia Tylzanowska

Charmaine Underwood
Brian Urbanik
Javier Uribe

Vincent van den Brink
Catherine Venart
Claudio Venier
Alan Vihant

Brent Wagler
Jeff Wagner
John Wall
Deborah Wang
Bruno Weber
Evan Webber
Chris Wegner
David Weir
Scott Wiseman
Matthew Wilson
Michael Wong
Richard Wong
Rufina Wu
Ricardo Wulff

Arlene Yee

Athos Zaghi
Paolo Zasso
Nick Zigomanis
Garth Zimmer

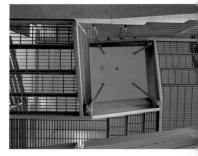

Afterword

A Conversation with Rodolphe el-Khoury

RODOLPHE eL-KHOURY: There is a growing sense of a particular Toronto architecture sensibility. It is perhaps most evident to visitors or outsiders like myself, who are struck by a common and distinct manner in much of the recent work in Toronto. Attempts to define or trace the genealogy of the so-called "Toronto School" invariably point to KPMB and to some of its landmark buildings in the city as a prime locus, if not to say origin, for the emergent sensibility. How would you characterize this shared sensibility? Do you see your own work shaping it?

Background

BRUCE KUWABARA: I think that you have to start with the fact that all four partners of KPMB worked for Barton Myers Associates. Barton Myers had been a partner of Jack Diamond. He had been educated at the University of Pennsylvania where Louis Kahn and Robert Venturi taught. Their firm, A.J. Diamond, Architect & Barton Myers, had an "outsider" impact on Toronto in the late

1960s and early 1970s. One of their first projects was York Square on the corner of Yorkville Avenue and Avenue Road, for the developer Richard Wookie.

Rather than tear down the existing Victorian houses on the site, they retained and renovated them. They added a new infill office and retail building behind them, creating an urban courtyard. It was an oasis in a desert at the time: a revelation; how to heal the tattered urban fabric that was a consequence of Toronto's overzealous modernist agenda in the post-war decades.

It is interesting to consider Woodsworth College in relationship to York Square and to see how this European model is transformed into one of the seminal projects of the practice. Remember that Woodsworth College was one of the projects that heralded the emergence of KPMB from Barton Myers Associates.

York Square used red brick and glass in a combination that created distinct, albeit, "pop" façades with round windows. The exist-

ing tree that was once in the backyard of one of the houses was retained and now is the centrepiece of the courtyard. So the first influence is Diamond and Myers as reform architects during a critical phase of development in Toronto in which a reform platform for politics and the city was advanced by a number of important figures including Jane Jacobs, Jim Lorimer, John Sewell and David Crombie. These policies supported the inclusion of mixed-uses in the inner city, the preservation of inner-city neighbourhoods, the strengthening of public transit, and the adaptive re-use of heritage buildings and the residual space between them.

The second influence is George Baird. I was part of George's small atelier office for three years along with Barry Sampson, Joost Bakker and John van Nostrand. The influence of George Baird on Toronto architects is very important. Not only is he influential as a teacher and critic, but also as an architect for whom several significant teachers/architects have worked. This group includes Don McKay, Brigitte Shim, Detlef Mertins, and historian Robert Hill.

The Baird studio produced two important studies related to urban design issues in Toronto. Both were used to support the City's landmark case at the Ontario Municipal Board to reform the zoning bylaw in 1975 with the intention of creating the mixed-use zoning bylaw. This was critical to the development of residential uses in the downtown. The studies included *Onbuildingdowntown* and *Built-Form Analysis*, a study of mixed-use building types.

Through the academic studios taught by Baird, issues concerning the architecture of the city emerged in a way that focused on urban morphologies and building typologies. This direction was developed in parallel to the approach developed and presented in the publication

Rational Architecture by European theorists and architects such as Leon Krier, Aldo Rossi, Matthias Ungers and Rafael Moneo.

The third impact on the work of the practice is James Stirling, along with his partner, Michael Wilford. Consider the design of Kitchener City Hall in relationship to Stirling's Neue Staatsgalerie in Stuttgart, particularly the diagonal path that cuts through the building, past the central void of the Civic Rotunda.

The fourth influence on the work of KPMB is what could be called Toronto Modern. By that I mean the work of modernists such as Peter Dickenson, Ron Thom and international architects such as Mies van der Rohe (in particular his Toronto Dominion Centre, 1963–67) and I.M. Pei (Canadian Imperial Bank of Commerce, 1972).

Emerging Shared Sensibility

The shared sensibility that has emerged in Toronto is driven by a number of factors. The first factor is the city itself, and the idea that contemporary architecture can support the vitality of the urban condition. Many of the Toronto projects respond to the urban context in interesting ways, such as searching for strategies of integration without simply mimicking what exists, specifically through a system of courtyards, covered walkways, alleys and interstitial spaces. In this sense, new architecture is positioned in an evolving dynamic relationship to the existing urban fabric — dynamic in that it is a revitalizing relationship.

The second characteristic is the use of materials, specifically masonry (stone and brick), wood and glass. The new architecture is focused on the exquisite detailing of material assemblage and tectonic expression. For stone and brick exterior walls, rain screen technology is employed. Windows are aluminum or wood and often operable. Glass is usually low-E type, with a minimum tint to reduce heat gain.

Formally, the projects are preoccupied with rectilinear geometries, sliding surfaces and floating planes. Spatially, the projects contribute to the formation of public squares, pedestrian streets and landscaped courtyards. Conventional, time-honoured urban spaces are re-interpreted in a contemporary way, and contribute to a more positive evolution of the city.

KPMB projects that characterize the "Toronto School" include Woodsworth College and King James Place. Other projects to be included in this category are Donald McKay's Park Road House (1992), Shim Sutcliffe Architects' Laneway House (1992), Oleson Worland's North Toronto Memorial Community Centre (1994), Kohn Shnier Architects' Erindale Student Centre (1999), Taylor Hariri Pontarini's McKinsey Building (2000) and Lett/Smith's Bader Theatre (2002) both at Victoria University, Baird Sampson Neuert's Prospect Cemetery and Mausoleum (2002), and Teeple Architects' Eatonville Library (2002).

Of these, one group emerges out of a tradition of masonry buildings and the work of Diamond and Myers and Ron Thom, while the other group relates to influences of international contemporary architecture, especially OMA, Office for Metropolitan Architecture.

Another aspect of our work is that many of the projects involve renovations and additions. The ways in which new architecture can be seen to act as an intervention on existing buildings is very interesting to us. So many great examples of this kind of work exist primarily in Europe where many contemporary projects are a combination of old and new construction.

We have completed a number of projects in Toronto that involve transforming existing building fabrics: Woodsworth College, the Munk Centre for International Studies and the Design Exchange. The pre-occupation with the design of the connecting elements including circulation spaces and stairs has become a significant dimension of our practice and work. I think that our interior projects always have an architectural idea behind them. The scale of spaces and elements is usually larger, framing the project of interior design as architecture. The tectonics of making interior space into interior architecture is consistent to our practice. For us, the high level of craft and the quality of materials has made renovations, interventions, additions and interiors legitimate acts of architecture.

Toronto now has an entire generation of architects who are interested in a neo-modernism of sorts. Neo-modernism is rounded out in the urban cosmopolitan matrix and is expressed as a fascination with material which is more artisanal and, if I may say, rural in appearance. I see a tension between the city and the country that is typical of Toronto and its rootedness in the rural culture of Ontario.

RODOLPHE eL-KHOURY: One of the striking features of KPMB's architecture — which, in my mind, accounts for much of the "Toronto style" is the way materials that have rich tactile qualities, the very materials we associate with craft and artisan work, are used in a language that speaks of abstraction and standardization, of mechanized and serial production. The materials evoke a vernacular building tradition in rural Ontario while the formal syntax and building morphology belong to urban culture. I am referring here to a constitutive contradiction or tension in the work that I also find typical of Torontonian identity: the

double and ambivalent allegiance to a rural past and a cosmopolitan present, a longing for authenticity in the rootedness of the Canadian landscape and a concomitant desire for the fluidity and artifice of urban culture. Is it then possible to think of the distinct flavour in KPMB — and by extension, in the "Toronto style" — as a manifestation of a firmly seated *mentalité*, as much as a consequence of international architectural trends and influences?

The Oscillation of Influences in Canadian Architecture

BRUCE KUWABARA: In *Pride of Place* (1986), Robert Stern argued that all American architecture, with the exception of the single-family house and skyscraper, was based on European precedents, transplanted and adapted to the social, economic and technological conditions of North America. Architectural design in Canada has always operated between European (French and English) and American influences. I also think that because of the differences between Canada and the United States in terms of politics, the social-democratic orientation of its society and outlook, that Canadian architects have always been more open to outside influences, especially in the context of increased globalization.

John Lyle (1872–1945) is one of the great Canadian architects. He designed Union Station, the Royal Alexandra Theatre, the concept for the Bank of Nova Scotia at King and Bay, and Central Presbyterian Church in Hamilton, where he was born. Lyle attended l'École des Beaux-Arts in Paris. He worked for a short period of time in New York doing renderings. When he returned, he tried to apply the lessons of the Beaux-Arts to his projects — composition, volumetric control, strong planning, stripped down classicism. With respect to ornamentation, Lyle tried to work with artisans and artists to create a system of representation that was authentically Canadian. So in his many designs such as for the Bank of Nova Scotia, Lyle introduced ornaments based on the flora and fauna of Canada on door pulls, on building surfaces, elevator doors, etc.

The reality and myth of the Canadian landscape has been identified as a major influence on Canadian architects such as Arthur Erickson, Ron Thom, the Patkaus, and Brigitte Shim and Howard Sutcliffe. But I think that KPMB's work has emerged more from an understanding of building typologies and morphologies, and less from landscape inspiration. At the same time our work seeks to respond to the harsh reality of the natural elements and the northern climate.

The multi-cultural composition of the City of Toronto is now recognized as one of its main characteristics. Toronto has attracted skilled fabricators and craftsmen particularly from Poland and the Czech Republic, but also from many other countries. I would also say that Toronto's construction industry is highly developed and highly skilled. So KPMB has managed to tap into a building culture that has excellent fabricators for millwork and miscellaneous metals, as well as larger construction companies that offer proficient construction and management services.

The early interiors projects (Marc Laurent, Nicolas, Dome Productions) enabled us to work very closely with specific materials — stone, wood, glass and metal — in an intensive and direct way. We were able to detail our work rigorously, almost at the level of industrial design. We learned about the issues of finishing, tolerances, industrial production and installation coordination from our fabricators. We were able to apply this knowledge to the design and fit-out of the interiors of our larger public buildings such as Kitchener City Hall.

In many of the public buildings, there was a desire, often expressed by our clients, to use local materials to represent the region or place. Again, with Kitchener City Hall, the building committee wanted us to use Canadian materials. The choice of the Red Indian sandstone which we had seen used on Arata Isozaki's MOCA building in Los Angeles was controversial. But the woods selected for the interior were oak and maple, and stones were black granite from Québec and Stanstead granite from New Brunswick.

So the preoccupation with real materials — stone and wood — and their use in combination with materials of industrial production — glass, steel, aluminum — was set going by our first interiors. The selection of stone and wood became an issue of representation and authenticity. The abstraction in the use of materials comes from our peculiar sense of scale. I think that our spaces and their built-in furnishings and millwork are often over-sized, giving them a slightly odd dimension.

We tend to use materials in a very simple and direct way to express their production qualities. For example, we would use veneered panels with an eye to maximizing the use of standard 2,400 sheet sizes. I think that we tend to design our millwork pieces as interventions within the base building.

We balance the desire for finely detailed elements with the use of certain materials in straight runs, maximizing repetition of the unit of construction. Many of our clients have commented on our use of material because it is not exactly normative. Tom's work is generally more robust, with husky dimensions. In some of the projects that I have been involved

with, the millwork elements play a significant role in shaping and inflecting space — for instance, in the Ravine House. Subtracting the millwork from the house would have a major impact on how the spaces read and interact.

One of the most influential projects for me was Pierre Chareau's Maison du Verre where the use of industrial products such as glass block and Pirelli rubber flooring was combined with steel framing, custom architectural bookshelves and stairs.

Barton Myers used off-the-shelf building elements in unconventional ways, in a design mode reminiscent of the Eames. Many of his buildings feature industrial building approaches with exposed systems. The Jackson-Triggs Winery revisits that direction by reinterpreting industrial and agrarian building types.

I think that our work can be distinguished by the oscillation between engagement with Canadian identity and international trends, between regional and local identity and global influence. I would like to think that we have resolved the conceptual tension that you have articulated by accepting oscillation and the hybrid condition of our office, and Canadian identity as our strategic mode of practice.

MARIANNE MCKENNA: There is a link to the political and economic shift of this country, as Toronto and Ontario emerged out of the Québec political crisis of the late 1970s as a stronger economic engine for Canada. Toronto was the city that benefited most from the economic surge of the late 1980s and the sustained growth of the 1990s. We started our practice in 1987 in that dramatic economic upswing. Institutional work was abundant and influenced by the overheated construction context: there were better budgets available for these buildings. This — coupled with the arrival of craftsmen from Europe (such as

Gregory Rybak from Poland who formed the millwork company MCM) — encouraged a material palette of exotic woods, metals and stone, a palette that leap-frogged beyond the brick and drywall of the earlier projects of Barton Myers and others in Toronto. It began with Woodsworth College, where instead of vandal-proof materials like vinyl composite tile floors and painted block walls mandated by the Physical Plant Department, KPMB shifted to a palette of French limestone floors, fir decking on the ceilings, polished plaster on the walls, custom door pulls with metal and wood, and sliding wood screens. People were amazed and delighted by the shift, and the project became a benchmark in our practice and in the university building boom of the 1990s.

RODOLPHE eL-KHOURY: Toronto's building culture of highly skilled fabricators indeed plays a great role in defining this architecture. You mention Gregory Rybak's MCM. If I am not mistaken, MCM is responsible for the millwork in buildings by Shim/Sutcliffe, Diamond and Schmitt, Hariri and Pontarini, and Ian MacDonald. These buildings represent radically different practices at vastly different scales, yet they exude the familial flavour we have been talking about. Is this culture rooted in a certain tradition and place threatened in any way by increasing globalization? Will it be sustained when skillfully crafted components become competitively available from other international sources? How will the CNC processes of fabrication that are changing the building industry influence the interplay between the standard and custom components you describe? How will KPMB's characteristic palette evolve with respect to ever proliferating new materials?

In short, how will KPMB sustain, or better yet, cultivate its hybrid identity in the context of new building economies and technologies?

BRUCE KUWABARA: We have been working with Gregory Rybak since 1990. The Toronto architects that you mentioned are alert to the quality of fabrication in projects of distinction within their community. Today Gregory's architectural millwork and metalwork is sold throughout North America.

I think that custom elements have the potential to be developed as standard components. A good example is in the area of lighting. We designed a custom direct/indirect lighting fixture for Kitchener City Hall which was fabricated by a company that immediately made our fixture as a catalogue item that others could purchase. I think this is not unusual as long as the production costs and demand allow the product to be marketable and commercially viable.

KPMB's characteristic palette of materials is constantly evolving. We are always looking for new materials to use in our projects. We have begun working with woven stainless steel fabrics in projects such as the Star Alliance Lounge in Zurich and the Genomics and Proteomics Research Building at McGill University in Montréal. We have also used cement board as an exterior cladding material in a rain screen application for the Jackson-Triggs Winery. We used blue acrylic panels and tinted glass in the James Stewart Centre for Mathematics at McMaster University. One of our working principles is to try to explore the use of different materials in every project.

I think that the new economies and technologies that will affect architecture in North America will emerge from an increasing demand for environmental sustainability in the built environment. European building systems and technologies are more advanced because the construction industry is responding to the longer standing movement to design

sustainable buildings, landscapes and cities. Sustainable design strategies have been developed with great sophistication and rigour in Europe as the result of the convergence of several forces: higher energy costs, the innovative spirit of the leading contemporary architects to integrate sustainability principles with outstanding architecture, pervasive social values and political leadership. I can see a future in which the rising costs of energy and the demand for environmental sustainability in North America will create the necessary momentum to change building practices. Standards related to environmental conditions and controls will change. European building products related to sustainability — including glazing technologies, solar shading systems — are now being marketed in North America.

In Europe, a Class A office building will be configured and designed to have natural ventilation, maximum day lighting, raised floors for wire management, indirect lighting, and careful material selection. Very few buildings in Europe are hermetically sealed. With increased sustainability, the responsibility for environmental control is shifted to the individual. The individual office worker decides whether to open a window, close a blind or turn on a light.

MARIANNE MCKENNA: Although our practice is stalwartly rooted in context, there is a strong signature backed by an obsessive desire to constantly innovate with materials, to inform each building typology as we are offered it — from elementary schools to prisons to geriatric residences — and to stimulate social interaction within the built form. In this way we are unrelenting. That said, we will be influenced by the global signature buildings, particularly as, within the next decade, we will watch a trio of them (Gehry, Libeskind and Alsop) go up

adjacent to our next generation of work in Toronto. I would predict that the expressive quality of the work will increase as both a response to the global influence and as a manifestation of competence and maturity. Recent buildings, like the Jackson-Triggs Winery, the Genomics and Proteomics Research Building at McGill and the HP Science and Technology Centre at Centennial College express the desire for a bigger image, but not at the expense of being unresponsive to program and site.

SHIRLEY BLUMBERG: Having built in Canada, the US and Europe now, we have come to appreciate and value even more the building culture in which we operate in Toronto. It is inextricably linked to the broader culture of a rapidly maturing city, an increasingly open, energetic and heterogeneous society. A recent issue of *The Economist* (27 September 2003) featured a leading article entitled "Canada's new spirit" where the writer declared that "a cautious case can be made that Canada is now rather cool." The article cites our social liberalism (legalized gay marriage, decriminalized marijuana) and lauds our "new spirit of risk-taking and experimentation."

There is a palpable feeling of anticipation in the city at this time. It feels as if the steady influx of immigrants over the last few decades has energized the city in a profound way. It feels more and more like it should — like living in a city state, an autonomous city that has become the cultural and economic engine for the country. Years of open immigration policy has produced a city that is extraordinarily diverse, richly textured and multi-cultural, animated and open in spirit. Toronto Artspace Inc. and the Canadian Urban Institute organized a conference entitled "Creative Places and Spaces: Strategies and Measures for Art

Growth and Urban Competitiveness" which attracted attendees from all over Canada, the US, Europe and Australia. Richard Florida and Jane Jacobs were featured speakers. Florida spoke of the culture of creativity and how a city's energy and creativity attracts the best and the brightest, fuelling the economy. With our local ground-up cultural groups flourishing, and the promise of a new Opera House, Art Gallery and Museum in the near future, Toronto seems to be growing more confident and mature.

Increasingly, globalization seems like an opportunity, not a threat. As we export our talents, so do our skilled millworkers and metalworkers export their innovative products. The CNC process of manufacturing has not only affected manufacturing, but also our work. For example, we used CNC to fabricate the three-dimensional model illustrating our design ideas for the Downsview Park Competition, which we did with Foreign Office Architects. New technologies and materials represent an expanded palette for our architecture, more ammunition for the preoccupations and explorations that have developed the hybrid condition in our work to date. The increasing international profile of our peers, the increasing sophistication of our building industry and the rigourous demands of practising sustainability in Canada have all contributed to a maturing confidence in the culture of architecture in Toronto.

Typeset in Whitman and Interstate by Richard Hunt, Archetype, Toronto
Printed and bound in Germany

Text editors: Ria Stein, Michael Wachholz (Birkhäuser); Kyo Maclear, Amanda Sebris, Norbert Sebris
Proofreaders: Kyo Maclear, Devorah Miller, Kave Rouhani, Amanda Sebris, Dawn Stremler

Cover Design: The Office of Kathleen Oginski, Toronto
Cover Photography: Tom Arban Photography, Toronto (front cover); Peter Sellar/KLIK, Oakville (back cover)
Endpaper Photography and Photo Essay Credits: pages 5–7, 22–41, 196–215: copyright Maris Mezulis, Toronto, 2004

"Toronto Style" by Detlef Mertins, Illustration Credits: page 15: Toronto City Hall, courtesy of Robert G. Hill; Toronto-Dominion Centre, Ron Vickers, photo courtesy of Toronto Dominion Bank Archives; page 16: O'Keefe Centre, image courtesy of the Robert G. Hill Collection; page 17: Scarborough College, University of Toronto, image courtesy of the Robert G. Hill Collection; drawing from the office of A. J. Diamond, Architect & Barton Myers, 1969, published in Walker Art Center, Design Quarterly No. 108 (1978); page 18: York Square, image courtesy of Ian R. Samson, Vancouver, B.C.; page 19: drawing by Paul Didur and John Stephensen from essay by George Baird in Design Quarterly No. 108 (1978).

Plates and Project Chronology Photography Credits:
Tom Arban Photography, Toronto: pages 152–153, 156, 157 (bottom), 169–175, 194, 195
Steven Evans, Toronto: pages 45, 47–49, 51–55, 57, 60 (top, left), 65, 67 (bottom row), 70, 75–77, 89–90, 192
Jeff Goldberg/ESTO, New York: pages 69, 71, 72–73, 79–81, 100–101, 146, 166–67, 192, 193, 195
Eduard Hueber, Arch Photo Inc., New York: pages 59–63, 107 (top row and bottom left), 108 (bottom), 109–111, 113, 114 (top), 115–116 (bottom), 120–121, 137 (bottom), 139, 141 (top), 142–143, 150 (top), 151, 154, 157 (top right), 158–165, 194, 195
Peter Sellar/KLIK, Oakville: pages 86–87 (top), 104–105, 106–107 (bottom left), 117–119, 131, 133–135, 145 (bottom), 147 (bottom), 149, 194

Additional Photography Credits:
Peter Aaron/ESTO, New York: page 94 (bottom), page 98 (top), page 194
Michael Awad, Toronto: pages 60 (bottom, lower right), 193, 194
Hedrich Blessing, Chicago: page 192
Michel Brunelle, Montréal: pages 137 (top), 138, 140–141 (bottom), 181, 195
Robert Burley, Design Archive, Toronto: pages 67 (top two rows), 114 (bottom), 116 (top), 193, 194
William Conley, Toronto: page 130
Ted Fahn, Copenhagen: page 126 (bottom)
Al Ferreira Photography, Hartford, CT: pages 145 (top), 147 (top)
Peter Gill, Toronto: pages 75, 193
Robert Hill, Toronto: page 60 (bottom, upper right)
Estate of Wolfgang Hoyt/ESTO, New York: page 45 (bottom row, right)
Kerun Ip, Toronto and Hong Kong: page 193
Walter Mair, Zurich: pages 103, 108 (top), 125–129, 194
Peter Paige, New Jersey: page 193
Chris Philips, Vancouver: page 98 (bottom)
Ben Rahn, A Frame, Toronto: pages 91, 179
Steve Rosenthal, Boston: page 192
Volker Seding, Toronto: pages 83, 193, 194
Martin Tessler, Vancouver: pages 92, 94 (top), 96–97, 98–99
Peter Wagner, Skylab Media, Toronto: pages 122–123
David Whittaker, Toronto: pages 85, 86 (bottom), 195

Many individuals contributed to the realization of this book. Special thanks to Tom Arban, Kevin Bridgman, Sylvain Bombardier, Sara Borins, Steven Casey, Robert Faber, Joan Gardner, Mitchell Hall, Daphne Harris, Eduard Hueber, Robert Hill, Richard Hunt, Norm Li, Ante Liu, Kyo Maclear, Maris Mezulis, Devorah Miller, Jason Mortlock, Kathleen Oginski, Johanna Radix, Paulo Rocha, Shabbar Sagarwala, Amanda Sebris, Norbert Sebris, Peter Sellar, Lola Skytt, Jeanna South, Ria Stein, Dawn Stremler, and Michael Wachholz.

Contributors:

Phyllis Lambert is founding director and chair of the board of trustees of the Canadian Centre for Architecture in Montréal, which she established in 1979 as an independent museum archive and architectural study centre. She has been recognized internationally for her contributions to contemporary architecture, and her role as an architect in the public realm. Her publications include Opening the Gates of Eighteenth-Century Montréal and Mies in America. Among the prizes she has been awarded are the 1997 Hadrian Award of the World Monuments Fund and the 2002 Chrysler Design Award.

Detlef Mertins is an architect, historian and critic known for his revisionist histories of modernism in the twentieth-century — in Canada, Europe and the United States. Having taught at the University of Toronto for many years, he is now Chair of the Architecture Department at the University of Pennsylvania. His publications include The Victory of the New Building Style, The Presence of Mies, and Metropolitan Mutations: The Architecture of Emerging Public Spaces.

Bruce Mau is creative director of the multi-disciplinary studio Bruce Mau Design in Toronto, which focuses on graphic, package, new media exhibition and 3D design. He is the recipient of the 1998 Chrysler Design Award and the 1999 Toronto Arts Award for Architecture and Design. His publications include S,M,L,XL, a compendium of projects and texts generated by Rem Koolhaas' Office for Metropolitan Architecture, and Life Style, a monograph on design culture and the work of the BMD studio.

Rodolphe el-Khoury is an architect, critic and historian. He is the Chair of Architecture at the California College of the Arts and principal of ReK Productions. He has authored, edited and translated several books in architecture and urban design, including Monolithic Architecture, Shaping the City: Studies in History, Theory and Urban Design and The Little House: an Architectural Seduction.